Poetry and Passion of the Lamb's War

This is an extraordinary piece of work. Presenting these epistles in poetic form breathes new life into them! This would be a wonderful read-aloud resource for meetings and gatherings.

—Chris Stern,
author of *Who Turned on the Light?: Stories of Hope and Healing*

George Fox wrote hundreds of epistles from the 1650s into the 1690s. Ben Richmond has sensitively collected and abridged the most significant of them into prose and poetry that makes their original power available to readers today.

—Thomas Hamm,
Emeritus Professor of History and
Quaker Scholar in Residence at Earlham College

Ben Richmond has made George Fox's epistles accessible to a new generation. After recognizing in them messages of comfort and of exuberant joy, as well as psalms of lament, Ben has put a selection into a poetic format, retitled some for clarification, added the context of the time when each was written and the scripture passages that gave them life. Foundational Quaker theology is a thread running through the commentary. This book would be useful for private devotion and very helpful for small group study.

—Margaret Fraser,
Ireland Yearly Meeting, and former executive secretary,
Friends World Committee for Consultation, Section of the Americas

Ben Richmond takes excerpts from Fox's epistles and renders them in poetic form in such a way that makes these old letters accessible to contemporary readers. We not only capture the essential messages but sense the beauty and music. The background information and biblical references put the letters in their original context and satisfy the need for a logical, historical understanding. The poetry touches our intuitive, emotional side, all leading to a holistic reading that can be transformative.

—Nancy Thomas,
author of *The Language of Light*

What a wonderful book. Ben Richmond brings the epistles of George Fox to life and makes them so accessible. A truly inspiring volume!

—Ben Pink Dandelion,
Professor of Quaker Studies, University of Birmingham

I would encourage readers who find George Fox's *Journal* hard going to turn to Ben Richmond's selections from his Epistles. You will discover how directly Fox's voice spoke to his contemporaries—and to us. This version, laying out the words in short and powerful lines, helps the reader to absorb them in a fresh and engaging way. And Ben's short comments give useful context and insights into the message.

—John Lampen,
author, *Wait in the Light: The Spirituality of George Fox*

This is a wonderful book! With great clarity and power, Ben Richmond brings George Fox's words to life, making them accessible and meaningful for us today, and in so doing, provides an invaluable primer on early Quaker spirituality and discipline. I hope this rich resource will be widely used for study and reflection by individual Friends and within Quaker communities for many years to come.

—Stuart Masters,
Quaker teacher at Woodbrooke, author, *The Rule of Christ: Themes in the Theology of James Nayler* and *The Quaker Faith: Friends of Love and Truth*

Four hundred years since his birth, George Fox's writings still speak with prophetic power and deep spiritual insight. Ben Richmond's collection of Fox's letters make his spiritual counsel accessible and vivid, by arranging them in verse form and offering pertinent introductory information and biblical references. Since Fox often dictated rather than wrote his letters, Richmond's verse-form captures the moment freshly. I recommend *Poetry and Passion* both to newcomers and to long-time listeners to Fox.

—Douglas Gwyn,
author, *Apocalypse of the Word: The Life and Message of George Fox* and *Seekers Found: Atonement in Early Quaker Experience*

Poetry and Passion of the Lamb's War

From the Epistles of George Fox

Excerpts selected and edited
Ben Richmond

With an introductory essay,
"On Poetry and Prophecy"
Paul N. Anderson

BARCLAY PRESS
Newberg, OR 97132

Poetry and Passion of the Lamb's War

From the Epistles of George Fox

Barclay Press, Inc.
Newberg, Oregon
www.barclaypress.com

Cover design: Mareesa Fawver Moss

Author photo: Jody Richmond

ISBN 978-1-59498-224-8

Printed in the United States of America.

The days of virtue, love, and peace
are come and coming,
and the Lamb had and has the kings of the earth
to war withal and to fight withal,
who will overcome
with the sword of the spirit,
the word of his mouth,
for the Lamb shall have the victory.

George Fox, Epistle 9

Contents

On Poetry and Prophecy—From the Lamb's War to Gospel Order in the Epistles of George Fox

Paul N. Anderson[1]

The writings of George Fox are voluminous, filling eight volumes in the 1831 collection of essays renamed in 1990 as *The Works of George Fox*, of which the final two volumes feature his epistles, letters, and testimonies.[2] Filling a total of 661 pages, that collection does not even include all the letters referenced in Fox's *Journal*, and while they are ordered chronologically, there's something to be said for gathering a selection of epistles on salient themes and subjects, allowing Fox's message back in the day to sink in for contemporary readers, as well.

And that is precisely what Ben Richmond has performed in gathering and editing this beautiful selection of Fox's letters on the subjects of "The Lamb's War" and "Gospel Order." Indeed, there are few themes as prophetic and important among the religious writings of the modern era as these, and as rendered in the epistles of George Fox, their meaning comes powerfully clear in this important new book.

---

1 Paul N. Anderson serves as Professor of Biblical and Quaker Studies, George Fox University, Newberg, Oregon, and as Extraordinary Professor of Religion at North-West University, Potchefstroom, South Africa.

2 *The Works of George Fox*, Vols. 7 and 8; Vols. I and II, Arthur Windsor (introducing the reprinting of 1831 edition; State College, Pennsylvania: New Foundation Publication, 1990).

While other collections of the epistles of George Fox have been gathered in the past, there has never been such a poetic and prophetic selection and rendering as this one.[3] In that sense, the present collection presents several features that make it well worthwhile for readers now and in the future.

First, privileging the genre of how the letters were composed and received, Richmond and others "listened" to the letters as well as reading them. If indeed Fox dictated his messages to a scribe, and if they were read aloud to their audiences, the practice of reading them out loud nowadays lends a sense of cadence and poetic structure that a mere silent reading cannot otherwise produce. That being the case, Richmond notes the strophic, repetitive structures of poetic verse, highlighting the oral-aural character of the letters' delivery and reception in the seventeenth century.

Like the Gospel of Mark, which was likely performed dramatically among early believers, "hearing" Fox's letters today lends a lively sense of how its original audiences may well have received them back in the day. Thus, I encourage people to read the letters out loud and then to reflect upon and discuss their content and emotive effect personally.

Second, Richmond performs a truly helpful service in listing referenced biblical texts alongside the messages of the letters. The King James (1611) version is presented in most instances, as it was presented as the "Authorized Version" of the day, although Puritans and some early Friends would have also read the Geneva Bible, and Fox himself donated a beautiful Coverdale Bible to Swarthmoor Hall, another favorite. Again, biblically well-versed believers in the seventeenth century would have been familiar with even terse biblical references, so having access to a full verse or paragraph illumines the larger contexts of authoritative allusions.

Third, in focusing on central gospel-themes in the preaching and ministry of George Fox, Richmond helpfully adds some of the "letters"

3 See, for instance, *Selections from the Epistles of George Fox*, Samuel Tuke, ed. (Providence, Rhode Island: Obadiah Brown Benevolent Fund, 1879); *No More but My Love: Letters of George Fox, 1624–1691*, Cecil W. Sharman, ed. (London: Quaker Home Service, 1980); *The Power of the Lord Is Over All: The Pastoral Letters of George Fox*, T. Canby Jones, ed. (Richmond, Indiana: Friends United Press, 1989).

and missives featured in his *Journal*, even if they are not included in the 1831 otherwise exhaustive *Letters* volumes of *The Works of George Fox*. This allows Richmond to add some of our favorite texts and quips by Fox, connecting them also with themes developed in his letters. This endeavor thus builds bridges between themes in various groupings of Fox's writings in ways that offer a fuller sense of his treatments of issues, especially the important ones upon which Richmond focuses.

Fourth, the thoughtful introductions to and commentaries upon the letters chosen alerts the reader to contextual issues behind particular themes being developed, offering fuller understandings of meanings then and now. For the investigative reader, these comments and notes allow one to go deeper into the subject addressed; for the associative reader, the commentary lends a fuller sense of meaning for each of the letters being featured. In Richmond's arrangement of the letters addressed, one also gets a sense of progressive development in Fox's communications as well as a feeling for the growth of particular issues among Friends of the day, both near and far.

As readers receive this new book published beautifully by Barclay Press, I encourage individuals and groups to once again perform the texts aloud in order to appreciate and feel the "first kiss" of the text. This can be seen as a reader-response approach. As the letters of George Fox reflect his dialogues with early Friends, we too are now drawn into fresh dialogues with George Fox himself. Aided also by Richmond's interpretive commentary and reminders of classic biblical texts, the words of the Russian form critic Mikhail Bakhtin come to mind:[4]

> There is neither a first word nor a last word. The contexts of dialogue are without limit. They extend into the deepest past and the most distant future. Even meanings born in dialogues of the remotest past will never be finally grasped once and for all, for they will always be renewed in later dialogue. At any present moment of the dialogue there are great masses of forgotten meanings, but these will be recalled again at a given moment in the dialogue's later course when

4 With these words, Bakhtin closed the last essay he ever wrote. *Dialogism: Bakhtin and his World*, Michael Holquist, ed. (London/New York: Routledge, 1984), p. 350.

> it will be given new life. For nothing is absolutely dead: every meaning will someday have its homecoming festival.

Having recently celebrated the 400th birthday of George Fox in 2024, these key themes in his life and witness are especially timely for today's seekers of truth, as well. For indeed, it is not we ourselves who have any hope in combating the trials and tribulations of the day; the victory is God's. The victory of the Lamb's War—over sin, injustice, and death—has already been accomplished. With the sacrificial declaration of the uplifted Lamb on the cross, "It is finished!" (John 19:30). We are thus invited to live into the blessed gospel order of love for God, neighbor, enemy, and even one another.

From poetry to prophecy, as we hear and read some of the most salient missives of George Fox, their meanings then and now produce a "homecoming festival" within us and among us. And this is why we can "sing and rejoice" as children of the day and of the light, "for the Lord is at work in this thick night." For indeed, "the power of the Lord God" is over all.

George Fox, 1624–1691

In mid-seventeenth-century England, George Fox inspired and then organized the radical Christian renewal movement known originally as "the children of Light." Called derisively, "Quakers," they adopted the name, Friends, based on Jesus' words, "Greater love has no one than this, that he lay down his life for his friends. You are my friends, if you do what I command" (John 15:13–14, NRS).

The context of Fox's life was civil war: a bloody struggle between authoritarian government claiming the divine right of kings and the parliamentary assertion of its authority as the representatives of the people. Each side of this struggle sought to establish their legitimacy in a national religion. The Quakers rejected national Christianity in favor of the spiritual authenticity of lives visibly transformed by the indwelling Light of Christ. They experienced the struggle of the Light against sin, first in individual integrity and inward righteousness, and then in the prophetic call for justice and equity in society. They called this struggle "the Lamb's war" (Revelation 17:14).

A Chronology

1624—George Fox is born at Drayton-in-the-Clay to Christopher Fox, and Mary Lago Fox "of the stock of the martyrs," a reference to the persecution of Protestants under Queen Mary a century earlier.

1625–1649—Reign of Charles I.

1642–1651—Civil War between the monarchy and Parliament.

1643—George Fox leaves home in search of religious authenticity.

1647—George Fox (twenty-three years old) begins his public ministry.

> And when all my hopes . . . in all men were gone, so that I had nothing outwardly to help me, . . . then, Oh then, I heard a voice which said, 'There is one even Christ Jesus, that can speak to thy condition', and when I heard it my heart did leap for joy (Ni:11).

1649—Charles I is put on trial by Parliament and is beheaded.
1649–1659—Oliver Cromwell, Lord Protector of the Commonwealth.
1649—George Fox suffers first of many imprisonments.
1650—George Fox claims to be free of sin because Christ has taken away his sin, and he is again imprisoned. Offered release contingent on accepting a captaincy in the Parliament's army, he refuses:

> I told them I lived in the virtue of that life and power that took away the occasion of all war (Ni:65).

1652—A "great people," the seekers of Westmorland, are convinced; the "Valiant Sixty" begin a campaign of preaching "the everlasting Gospel" throughout England and abroad.
1660—Charles II returns from exile and is restored to power.
1661—George Fox and other leading Quakers issue the peace testimony:

> All bloody principles and practices, we . . .do utterly deny; with all outward wars and strife and fightings with outward weapons, for any end or under any pretence whatsoever (Ni:399).

1662—The Quaker Act requires an oath of loyalty: thousands of Friends are imprisoned in obedience to Jesus' command, "swear not at all" (Matthew 5:34).
1667 onward—George Fox focuses on organizing men's and women's monthly and quarterly meetings.
1669—George Fox and Margaret Fell marry.
1671–1973—George Fox travels in the Caribbean and North America.

1689—William and Mary are crowned; they promulgate a bill of rights and the Act of Toleration (for Protestants), ending much of the persecution of Quakers and other Protestant dissenters.

1691—George Fox dies, aged sixty-seven years.

Introduction

I started reading the epistles of George Fox as a devotional exercise and found his words deeply moving.

> The days of virtue, love and peace
>   are come and coming (Epistle 9).

Who does not yearn to be part of a movement as dynamic and uplifting as that?

But I also found Fox's seventeenth-century English was sometimes obscure, his style dense and repetitive. When it occurred to me to take one of the difficult passages and reformat it, a lovely poem emerged. I began to hear the cadences of a powerful preacher. I could imagine Fox dictating these letters in the evenings as he and his companions rested from their travels—or perhaps as they sat in prison for their faith. Rather than studying these letters as essays, I began to listen to them as part of an oral tradition—spoken aloud to small groups who gathered together to hear the insights of a modern-day apostle.

Some of what I heard surprised me. For instance, I was surprised by this strikingly contemporary warning: "a man that . . . runs into debt, and lives highly . . . is not serviceable . . . but a destroyer of the creation" (Epistle 200). This made me think not only of the high rate of consumer debt but of fund managers leveraging debt to build huge corporations, and the destruction of creation resulting in the crisis of climate change. I was also surprised how central was care for the poor to his vision: Quaker business meetings were to "see that nothing be lacking" (Epistle 264, Pt c).

And that if any Friends
be oppressed any manner of way,
others may take care to help them (Epistle 121).

Even more surprising, this concern extended beyond his own community. Fox urged Friends, "seek out the poor, and sick, and fatherless, and widow[s], and imprisoned, and make up their necessities and wants" (Epistle 175). There is a worthy agenda item for our business meetings!

I was also surprised by the vehemence of Fox's denunciation of deceit. "Loathe deceit and all unrighteousness" (Epistle 200). This included a concern that Friends should speak truthfully, but Fox clearly had something bigger in mind: "Set up truth, and confound the deceit" Fox urges in Epistle 55; "Lay the sword upon it" he writes to Friends in public ministry in his "Walk Cheerfully" letter. Today, deceivers confound our dignity as children of God by reducing us to cogs in a corporate economy, identified chiefly as "consumers." Liars in the political sphere seek to divide us by nationlity, gender, race, and offer the false hope of security, even nobility, through raw power and escalating violence.

The struggle against all this is the "war of the Lamb." The task is to free people who are spiritually imprisoned by deceit, and the goal is the glorious freedom of the children of God.

For the lamb must have the victory,
mark, the lamb, and not the rough nature
which hath gotten up since man fell from God's image.
(Epistle 101)

Listening to Fox, I feel the importance of being spiritually formed in a community that follows the Lamb rather than "the rough nature."

Most of all, in these letters, we hear the counsel, comfort, and exhortation, of "a lover of your souls" (Epistle 205), inviting people everywhere to enter a new life. For Fox, the worst deceit was the idea that true goodness was impossible in this life. Rather, as we come to believe in the Light within us, he says, we come to know Christ dwelling in us—"Christ in you, the hope of glory" (Colossians 1:27, KJV). Now co-heirs with Christ, how can we fail to be transformed by God's goodness and love?

Salvation cannot be reduced to the assertion of certain doctrinal truths. Nor should salvation be reduced to hope for eternal life when we die. To Fox, that is professing faith without the power of it. Fox also warns against relying on the outward trappings of a peculiar Quaker process or lifestyle. This he calls mere "imitation" (Epistle 47). The Quaker testimonies, considered as teachings and practices, have no power in themselves to "answer that of God" in others but do so only as they testify to "the life" within. Therefore, Fox, over and over again, invites us to "wait for" and "dwell in" the life, the love, and the power of God. There is the source of authentic, counter-cultural Christianity.

Here is real transformation that can only be expressed in the language of myth where the deep truths may be found. Time and again, Fox returns to the metaphor of being brought by Christ into "the state of Adam and Eve before the fall" (e.g., Journal Ni:27; Epistles 239, 262, 308). Fox offers rich organic metaphors, such as being "grafted into Christ" who is "the living tree" (Epistle 354), and to live in "in the light, which was before darkness was" (Epistle 163). If we dwell in the Light, we receive "power to become children of God" (John 1:12). If we allow ourselves to be ruled by God's wisdom and love, we will be drawn into fellowship with others and begin to transform the world. A transformed life, marked by the goodness and love of God and unity with others, is a sign of salvation, a testimony to the power of God.

We need to listen for the living Word of God, spoken inwardly in the heart. This was the essence of the "worship in spirit and in truth" (John 4:24, KJV) that Jesus set up and was now being revived amongst the Quakers (Epistle 222). It was essential to wait together in silence to "feel the seed of God among you all, though never a word be spoken" (Epistle 77). But silence is not an end in itself; the point is to give the Spirit freedom to move in power. I think we may have lost a sense of how much fun was to be had. For instance, I was surprised to find, in at least a dozen of his letters, Fox encouraging singing in the Spirit:

as they are moved by the spirit
to pray, to praise, to give thanks,
to speak with the spirit,

as it gives utterance,
as it reveals things,
and so it leads them. . . .

Now he that hath a psalm,
(mark,) now he that hath one,
let him sing, and sing in the spirit,
and with understanding. (*To All People on the Earth*)

From time to time, as in Epistle 38, I think we can hear Fox, himself, filled with the joy the Spirit, bursting into song:

O happy day! praises! praises!
Praise ye the Lord, ye righteous ones;
sing praises to the Lord God Almighty for ever!

It gives me joy to listen for the melodious movements of the Word in Fox's letters. His poetry reminds us that we must never try to reduce the life in the Spirit to logical propositions. Rather, let us join hands and revel together in its power and holy passion.

The glorious Light is shining
the immortal is bringing forth out of death,
the prisoners have hope of their pardon,
the debt being paid
and they freely purchased by Christ's blood.

He into the prison house is come,
that the prisoners begin to sing
in hope of their eternal freedom,
for joy of heart leaping,
and the dumb tongue shall sing praises.
(Epistle 27)

Sources

This is a collection of excerpts from Fox's epistles. For each Epistle, I have provided a short introductory note and one or more Bible verses. For these, I have generally used either the King James Authorized Version (1611) or the Geneva Bible (1599), which are the versions Fox seems to most closely echo in his epistles. For the full text of the epistles, I have relied on the 1831 edition of Fox's Works, as found on the Digital Quaker Collection hosted by the Earlham School of Religion website. I have taken care to indicate by ellipses where I have omitted words. The formatting as poetry is mine. Words in square brackets are mine. Bolding is mine. Italics in the epistles are from Fox's Works. The titles of the epistles are mine unless noted.

The table of epistles in numerical order may help the reader navigate Fox's text.

I make reference to T. Canby Jones, ed., *The Power of the Lord Is Over All: The Pastoral Epistles of George Fox*, Friends United Press, 1989 (cited here as Jones:[page]). Edited for length and clarity, it is invaluable as the only collection of all Fox's epistles currently in print. I also refer to the *Journal of George Fox*, edited by John Nickalls, London, Religious Society of Friends, 1975 (cited as Ni:[page]). Partway through my project, I encountered Terry H. S. Wallace's sensitive treatment of selections from Fox's epistles *QuakerPsalms: A Book of Devotions*, Foundation Publications, 2002; and *Have Salt in Yourselves: A Book of QuakerPsalms*. Foundation Publications, 2010. For help with earlier meanings of words, I referred to *The Compact Edition of the Oxford English Dictionary*, Oxford University Press, 1971, cited as OED. For historical background, I found useful Jonathan Healey, *The Blazing World: A New History of Revolutionary England, 1603–1689,* Knopf, 2023, Kindle ed. (cited as Healey:[page]).

Acknowledgments

Many thanks to Friends who read and commented on an early draft of this work. Notably, this includes Jody Richmond, whose detailed reading and re-reading of my comments and Fox's epistles should qualify her for equal billing as my co-editor and I dedicate this book to her.

Thanks also to Judy Maurer and Doug Gwyn, whose comments on an early draft have made it better, and to Paul Anderson for his encouragement and helpful introductory essay. Thanks also to Eric Muhr and all at Barclay Press whose vision for this book sharpened my own and brought the manuscript to light.

I dedicate this work also to Margaret Jump, now deceased. I count her as my "mother in Quakerism" (see Epistle 291). When I joined Friends through Multnomah Monthly Meeting (Portland, Oregon) in the early 1970s, she gave me a precious copy of *A Day-book of Counsel & Comfort from the Epistles of George Fox,* compiled and published in 1937 by Lucy Violet Hodgkin. Though even then it was long out of print, it consolidated in me a conviction that true life is to be found in the Light of Christ within.

A word about words

Fox was far ahead of his time in advocating the equality of men and women (see, for instance, Epistles 249 and 320), and he was often careful to use inclusive phrases such as "the witness of God in all men and women" (Epistle 123). But, as was standard until recent times, he also uses "man" to encompass all humanity. I have let Fox's words stand.

Where Fox uses words that have become obsolete or changed in meaning, I have tried to note that in the introductions. For instance:

> "lust" has come to be associated only with improper sexual desire but in earlier times could be applied to any passionate interest;
>
> "who" which Fox sometimes uses as a relative pronoun, where we would say, "that one," or sometimes as an indefinite pronoun where we would say, "whoever";

"withal" has entirely dropped out of use, but in Fox's time was the form properly used when "with" came at the end of a phrase.

"heathen" occasionally appears in the epistles or scriptures. The King James Version almost always so translates the Hebrew word *goy* which actually means any non-Jewish people or nation. Although Fox seems sometimes to be captive to the dominant culture of white superiority, his theology is inclusive and egalitarian, as shown for instance here:

> and God, who made all,
> pours out of his spirit
> upon all men and women in the world,
> in the days of his new covenant,
> yea, upon whites and blacks,
> Moors, and Turks, and Indians,
> Christians, Jews, and Gentiles. (Epistle 388)

In the text of the epistles, I have retained the spelling, capitalization, and (for the most part) the punctuation found in Fox's *Works.* This includes two occasions when Fox uses the non-standard spelling, "Swarthmore," for Margaret Fell's home, Swarthmoor Hall.

Ben Richmond
January 24, 2024

Part One:
The Poetry and Passion of the Lamb's War

Now was I come up in spirit through the flaming sword into the paradise of God. All things were new, and all the creation gave another smell unto me than before, beyond what words can utter. I knew nothing but pureness, and innocency, and righteousness, being renewed up into the image of God by Christ Jesus, so that I say I was come up to the state of Adam, which he was in before he fell. . . . But I was immediately taken up in spirit, to see into another or more steadfast state than Adam's in innocency even into a state in Christ Jesus, that should never fall. And the Lord showed me that such as were faithful to him in the power and light of Christ, should come up into that state in which Adam was before he fell.

George Fox, *Journal* for 1648 (Ni:27)

And so be of good faith and valiant for the truth:
for the truth can live in the jails.
And fear not the loss of the fleece,
for it will grow again;

and follow the lamb,
if it be under the beast's horns,
or under the beast's heels;
for the lamb shall have the victory
over them all.

Epistle 227

The Light that Enlightens Everyone

The true light, which enlightens everyone,
was coming into the world.
John 1:9 (NRS)

To All People on the Earth (Works 4:119ff, 1657)

Introductory Note

The starting point was Fox's experience in 1647: "then, Oh then, I heard a voice which said, 'There is one, even Christ Jesus, that can speak to thy condition,' and when I heard it my heart did leap for joy" (Ni:11). It is possible for people to hear the voice of God speaking within. But to hear, Fox says, we must first come to the silence. To be silent, we must come out of the "bustling"—a word from Fox's day that describes so well the ways we fill our time with activity that in the end has little true meaning but is concerned solely with outward business and position. In the midst of all this hustle and bustle, Fox calls Friends—and, through them, the whole world—to silent waiting and into the life that really matters. In the silence, Fox promises us healing from life's hurts and the glory of connection with God.

These excerpts from a longer epistle emphasize the drumbeat of Fox's invitation "to all." God's grace is not for a select few. All can enjoy a more authentic life. This epistle is found in Works of George Fox (4:119–135). In true seventeenth-century style, its original title attempted to summarize the whole: *An Epistle to All People on The Earth; Shewing the Ignorance of all the World, both Professors and Teachers, of the Birth that must be Silent, and of the Birth that is to Speak, which declares God; and the Difference betwixt Silence and Speaking, that they may come to an Understanding of themselves, and may know that Christ Jesus, the Light of the World, is their Teacher, or their Condemnation: Also shewing that it was the Practice of many to wait in Silence upon God, to hear his Word, and know his Voice. —By G. F.*

Fox instructed, "This is to be read amongst Friends, and from them to pass abroad through the world." (4:123) This was seventeenth-century reposting content—starting with Friends in hope of reaching ever wider circles until everyone is included.

Note: at the end of this epistle, Fox gives the delightful appendix: *Something Farther Concerning Silent Meetings*. "Farther," (like "further") is used here to denote something additional that goes beyond what has been said before (see OED).

Scripture

Behold, the days come, saith the LORD, that I will make a new covenant. . . . I will put my law in their inward parts, and write it in their hearts; and will be their God, and they shall be my people. And they shall teach no more every man his neighbour, and every man his brother, saying, Know the LORD: for they shall all know me, from the least of them unto the greatest of them, saith the LORD: for I will forgive their iniquity, and I will remember their sin no more.

Jeremiah 31:31, 33–34 (KJV)
c.f., Hebrews 8:10–12; 10:16–17, 19–20

To every *thing there is* a season, and a time to every purpose under the heaven: . . . a time to keep silence, and a time to speak.

Ecclesiastes 3:1, 7 (KJV)

Epistle

[Come out of the Turmoil and Strife]

You are not come to know the time to keep silence before the time to speak, *Eccles.* 3. 7. . . . but the Lord will put you to silence, and you must witness silence before you come to speak. . . .

[T]here stands all the world, . . . every one striving for mastery and lordship and authority one over another: but it shall not be so with you who are children of light, disciples of Christ, not of this world, whose kingdom is not of the world, and who come out of strife, come into peace. Therefore . . .

Come out of the bustlings
you that are bustling
and in strife one against another,
whose spirits are not quieted,
but are fighting with words,
whose hearts burn against each other
with a mad blind zeal,

who are up in your wantonness, lightness and pleasures,
who set the whole course of nature on fire,
among whom the way of peace,
and that which is perfect is not known; . . .

where is all the masteries and seeking for earthly crowns,
and exalting among the people,
and gathering parties out of people;

wherein stand the several ways and distances of people one from another, . . .
destroying the meek of the earth and the helpless,
and rooting out innocency and simplicity, and destroying it. . . .

So there are all the unquiet spirits in the world, and the restless and the wearied . . . to have rest in Christ . . .; and such shall find mercy of God, when their minds are guided up unto God, and their spirits and minds are quieted in silent waiting upon God, and in one half hour have more peace and satisfaction, than they have had from all other teachers of the world all their life time. . . .

[Learn to Wait upon the Light.]

[A]ll people come to know
Christ your teacher,
who saith, learn of me,
I am the way to the Father;

so the light that doth enlighten
every one that cometh into the world,
is the new and living way; . . .

therefore all people come to know
the light in you, shining in your hearts,
to give you the knowledge of God,
in the face of Jesus Christ; . . .

and all people come
to know the new covenant
that God hath prophesied of by his prophets,

and Moses wrote of, and the apostles
were witnesses and enjoyers of,
the everlasting covenant . . .

and all people come to know
Christ in you the hope of glory, . . .
which hope purifies,
even as he is pure. . . .

[Wait in Silence and Speak with the Spirit]

All the world's teachers, people, and professors,
you are far from silence,
and the silent meeting together,
and waiting upon the Lord in silence,

you have too much flesh in you,
which speaks,
and so are too full of words . . .
        to hear his still voice. . . .

But a silent meeting is not a strange thing to [the] righteous . . . who do silently and patiently wait upon God for counsel, for instruction, who is the giver of all good; so

as they are moved by the spirit
to pray, to praise, to give thanks,
to speak with the spirit,
as it gives utterance,
as it reveals things,
and so it leads them. . . .

Now he that hath a psalm,
(mark,) now he that hath one,
let him sing, and sing in the spirit,
and with understanding.

And now he that sings in the spirit,
and prays in the spirit,
as the spirit gives utterance,
he is in that birth,
that silenceth the birth of the flesh.

And this is to all that would learn silent waiting upon God . . .

Keep to that of God in you,
which will lead you up to God,
when you are still from your own thoughts
and imaginations, and desires
and counsels of your own hearts,
and motions, and will;

when you stand single from all these,
waiting upon the Lord,
your strength is renewed;

he that waits upon the Lord,
feels his shepherd,
and he shall not want:

and that which is of God within every one,
is that which brings them together
to wait upon God,

which brings them to unity,
which joins their hearts together
up to God. . . .

Something Farther Concerning Silent Meetings

Concerning silent meetings;

the intent of all speaking
is to bring into the life,
and to walk in, and to possess the same,

and to live in and enjoy it,
and to feel God's presence,
and that is in the silence,

(not in the wandering whirling tempestuous part of man or woman)

for there is the flock
lying down at noon-day,
and feeding of the bread of life,
and drinking at the springs of life,
when they do not speak words;

for words declared are to bring people to it,
and confessing God's goodness and love,
as they are moved by the eternal God
and his spirit, . . .

in which the fellowship is attained to
in the spirit of God,
in the power of God,
which is the gospel,
in which is the fellowship,
when there are no words spoken.

The Light that Condemns (Epistle 6, 1652)

Introductory Note

The great news that the Light within every person has the capacity to lead all people without exception up to God, has a corollary which is that the Light is the condemnation to everyone who "walks contrary to it." This was often how people first experienced the Light. This condemnation is not human "scolding" but an inner response to the Light, which by its nature, reflects the purity and goodness of God. Friends often affirm "that of God in everyone," but the first action of the Light is to expose all that which is not of God in us.

Note: This, often painful encounter, is what Fox called "convincement." The OED gives this pertinent definition: "Conscientious or religious conviction; conviction of sin; esp. used by Quakers in the sense of religious conversion."

Scripture

And this is the condemnation, that light is come into the world,
and men loved darkness rather than light, because their deeds
were evil. For every one that doeth evil hateth the light, neither
cometh to the light, lest his deeds should be reproved.
John 3:19–20 (KJV)

Epistle

No one is justified,
breaking the commands of Christ;
no one is justified, living in iniquity

and no one is justified
in professing only Christ's words,
and the prophet's and the apostle's words,
and living out of their lives:

and no one is justified
living in the first birth and nature,
and false faith and hope,
which doth not purify, as God is pure.

No man is justified
not believing in the light as Christ commands,
but with the light is condemned;

for the light is the condemnation
of all them that walk contrary to it:
therefore the power of God mind.

No man is justified,
acting contrary to that spirit
which doth convince them.

Stand Still in Trouble (Epistle 10, 1652)

Introductory Note

The painful experience of convincement (Epistle 6) becomes good news when we continue to wait in the Light. "Then power comes." Power for what? Truly, that is the topic of all the epistles, but at its heart, Fox is speaking about the power to live free from everything "that is not of God in us." For those whose faults have been revealed by the Light, Fox says, "Do not think, but submit." Submission to the Light brings an inflowing of spiritual power by which we become children of God (see John 1:12–13, which Fox quotes in Epistle 45).

In this epistle, we hear Fox take a biblical story—the deliverance of the Hebrews from Pharoah's army at the Red Sea—and read it as a "figure" (an example) of a contemporary spiritual experience. During the Exodus, when the Hebrew people were trapped by Pharoah's army at the Red Sea, God told them not to be afraid because God would fight for them, and their role was simply to "stand still." In Fox's re-telling, Pharoah's army becomes a symbol for all "the thoughts and temptations" that separate us from God, and "standing still in the Light" is where we experience the inward war of the Lamb.

Note: at the Red Sea, the Israelites "stood still" as a community. How does the fact that waiting in the Light is a spiritual discipline Friends do together seem different than personal meditation?

Note also that the expression, "whatever ye are addicted to," can refer to any strong attraction as, for instance, a national addiction to fossil fuels.

Scripture

And Moses said unto the people, Fear ye not, stand still, and see the salvation of the LORD, which he will shew to you to day: for the Egyptians whom ye have seen to day, ye shall see them again no more for ever. The LORD shall fight for you, and ye shall hold your peace.
Exodus 14:13–14 (KJV)

But as many as received him, to them gave he power to become the sons of God, even to them that believe on his name.
John 1:12 (KJV)

Epistle

Whatever ye are addicted to,
the tempter will come in that thing;
and when he can trouble you,
then he gets advantage over you,
and then ye are gone.

Stand still in that which is pure,
after ye scc yourselves;
then Mercy comes in.

After thou seest thy thoughts, and the temptations,
do not think but submit,
and then Power comes.

Stand still in the Light and submit to it,
and the other will be hushed and gone;
and then content comes.

And when temptations and troubles appear,
sink down in that which is pure,
and all will be hushed, and fly away.

Your strength is to stand still, after ye see yourselves;
whatsoever ye see yourselves addicted to,
temptations, corruption, uncleanness, &c.

then ye think ye shall never overcome.
And earthly reason will tell you,
what ye shall lose; hearken not to that,

but stand still in the light that shows them to you,
and then strength comes from the Lord,
and help contrary to your expectation.

If ye do any thing in your own wills, then ye tempt God;
but stand still in that power
which brings peace.

The Dew of Heaven (Epistle 27, 1653)

Introductory Note

Fox begins this epistle with a celebration of the mystical unity of the community—male and female—"naked and bare" (we might say, transparent) before God. The imagery of the "dew of heaven" and release from the "prison house" are both evocative of God's blessing and gift of new life. Fox's image of prisoners singing praises for their deliverance from bondage causes me to wonder if sometimes Quakers in those early "silent" meetings might have burst forth in spontaneous songs of joy?

Fox's phrase, "the arrows of the Almighty are shooting against the wicked," comes from the prophet Zechariah, immediately following the prophecy of a meek and just king who comes riding on an ass, and declaring peace—the inspiration of Jesus' entry into Jerusalem riding on a donkey. Could Fox have seen the "arrows of the Almighty" in the Quakers engaged in the nonviolent war of the Lamb?

Scripture

The next day John seeth Jesus coming unto him, and saith, Behold the Lamb of God, which taketh away the sin of the world.
John 1:29 (KJV)

Therefore God give thee of the dew of heaven,
and the fatness of the earth,
and plenty of corn and wine.
Genesis 27:28 (KJV)

Behold, thy King cometh unto thee: he *is* just, and having salvation; lowly, and riding upon an ass . . . the battle bow shall be cut off: and he shall speak peace unto the heathen. . . . As for thee also, by the blood of thy covenant I have sent forth thy prisoners out of the pit. . . . Turn you to the strong hold, ye prisoners of hope: . . . And the LORD shall be seen over them, and his arrow shall go forth as the lightning.
Zechariah 9:9–12, 14 (KJV)

Epistle

To all my dear Friends and brethren every where. . . . Praises be unto the glorious God for ever, who has sent his son into the world, to take away the sins of the world.

The lamb of God,
the son of God,
is but one

in all his males and females,
sons and daughters,

and they all are one in Christ
and Christ one in them all.

And all Friends, . . . dwell all in the pure spirit of God. . . . [I]t will teach you every one in particular, to . . . stand naked and bare, and uncovered before the living Lord God . . . to receive instruction and counsel from him.

So God Almighty be with you all!

The dew of heaven is falling upon you
  to water the tender plants;
and the blessing of God be amongst you,
  which showers down amongst you!

The heavenly joy fill your hearts
  and comfort you in the inward man
  in all tribulations.

The glorious Light is shining,
  the immortal is bringing forth out of death,
the prisoners have hope of their pardon,
  the debt being paid
  and they freely purchased by Christ's blood.

He into the prison house is come,
  that the prisoners begin to sing
in hope of their eternal freedom,
  for joy of heart leaping,
  and the dumb tongue shall sing praises.

And the arrows of the Almighty
  are shooting against the wicked.

Therefore, be bold
and valiant for the truth,
triumph over all the deceivers,
and trample upon their deceits.

Mind the Steadfast Guide (Epistle 31, 1653)

Introductory Note

The Quaker spiritual journey is not that of a solitary pilgrim who hopes to find heaven after death. Rather, its goal is reached in this life: an experience of oneness with God that transforms, so that "we meet in the eternal spirit." In this epistle, we hear Fox's understanding of baptism and communion as spiritual realities by which it is possible for all people to be made "perfect."

It is worth taking some time to meditate on the closing verses, as Fox describes stages of Christ's rule: "waiting / for the coming of our Lord Jesus Christ / in you all / who is Lord over all, / to be Lord over all in you." In this short epistle, Fox shows the power of an inward and spiritual understanding of baptism, communion, and the "second coming."

Scripture

For by one Spirit are we all baptized into one body,
whether *we be* Jews or Gentiles, whether *we be* bond or
free; and have been all made to drink into one Spirit.
1 Corinthians 12:13 (KJV)

Epistle

Dear Friends,—

Mind the steadfast guide to the Lord,

where we do all meet in the eternal spirit,
  in oneness,

all being baptized by it into one body,
having one food, the eternal bread of life,
  which the immortal feed upon,

and all made to drink into one spirit,
which is the cup of the communion
  of the blood of our Lord Jesus Christ,

which makes perfect,
and redeems from all that is vain,
  fleshly, and earthly,

up to God, who is holy,
pure, spiritual,
  and eternal.

And let not any of you
in your desires wander from that
  which is pure in you;

then your conditions
will be kept clear and pure
  to see all things as they are,

and a clear separation will be made
from that which is of man, and of your own,
  and that which is of God;

and there will be a growing up
  in that which is pure.

And so, be low in your minds,

  waiting

for the coming of our Lord Jesus Christ
  in you all,

who is Lord over all,
    to be Lord over all
    in you.

And so the Lord God of power keep you all! Farewell.

Christ Is with Us in Temptations (Epistle 45, 1653)

Introductory Note

From time to time, Fox shares his own vulnerability. In this excerpt, he confesses to periods of despair in which he was tempted to "make himself away." Fox tells us that it is precisely in these times of hardship that we find fellowship with Christ who "has gone before and is able to succour us." The danger is to "lust after the creature" and "give way to the lazy, dreaming mind."

Note how Fox uses passages from John and Hebrews to illuminate the role of Jesus Christ. (The citations in square brackets are my addition.) It is also worth meditating on the closing passage in which Fox brings together the "mystery" of the "power" to receive the "second birth" and how this power contrasts with the devil's power.

This epistle was originally titled, *Concerning the heirs of the kingdom of God, and how Christ was, and his saints are tempted.*

Note: "Lust" in the usage of Fox's time referred to any human delight or passion. The OED gives an amusing example, the "lust [to] heare sermons."

Scripture

Then the devil took Him into the holy city; and he had
Him stand on the pinnacle of the temple, and said to Him,
"If You are the Son of God throw Yourself down."
Matthew 4:5 6 (RSV)

And forgive us our sins; for we also forgive every one that is indebted to us. And lead us not into temptation; but deliver us from evil.
Luke 11:4 (KJV)

That I may know him, and the power of his resurrection, and the fellowship of his sufferings, being made conformable unto his death.
Philippians 3:10 (KJV)

Epistle

[H]e was in the wilderness, and there
he was tempted to lust after the creature;
he was tempted to make himself away;
he was tempted to worship the devil,
(to bow down and worship him.)

He is the captain of our salvation; [Heb 2:10]
he is gone before,
he endured the cross,
he despised the shame,
he suffered the contradiction of sinners, [Heb 12:12]

for the glory that was set before him, [Heb 12:2]
he hath won the crown.
He hath overcome Egypt,
and he hath fulfilled the law,
he hath overcome the world, [John 16:33]
he hath overcome the temptations;
he is able to succour all who are tempted.

It is no sin to be tempted, but to enter into the temptation, that is sin. . . .

And Jesus Christ is the way, the truth, and the life, [John 14:6]
the door, that all must pass through, [John 10:7, 9]
and he it is, that opens it;
the same door that ever was
the same Christ yesterday, to day, and for ever.
[Heb 13:8]

Ye that have been in the wilderness, can witness this with me, and the same temptations, even to despair, and to make themselves away. . . . But it is no sin to be tempted; but standing in the power of the Almighty God, ye will be enabled to stand against, and above all the wiles of satan. So dwell in the power of Almighty God. . . .

So, examine yourselves,
    and see if ye have fellowship
    with Christ in his sufferings,
    and be brought to be comformable to him
    in his death,

and to have fellowship with him
    in his temptations and reproaches,
    and buffetings, and scornings,
    and the contradiction of sinners,
    and to be spit upon, as he was;

and he that hath fellowship with him in his sufferings,
    shall have fellowship with him in his glory.
And he that doth confess him in this dark world,
    him will he confess before his Father, and his
      angels. . . .

[B]eware ye enter not into the temptation,
to lust after the creature,
and give not way to the lazy, dreaming mind,
for it enters into the temptations.

So there thou wilt be polluted
with the pollutions of the world;
then thou wilt be tempted to despair,
and the devil there gets power upon thee,
if thou enter into temptations, and follow thy imaginations
in going from the light of Christ within thee. . . .

And all who can witness the second birth, and are born again, . . . ye come up to God, who was before time was. This is a mystery, he that can receive it let him. . . .

And as many as received Christ,
he gave power to them
to become the sons of God,

which are not born by the will of man,
but by the will of God;
not by water only,
but by water and the spirit.

Dwell in That Which Is Pure (Epistle 50, 1653)

Introductory Note

Here is a partial guide to Quaker spiritual practice. Three times, Fox uses the phrase, "dwell in that which is pure," followed by the instruction to "wait." This suggests three aspects of waiting that Fox wants us to look at: (I) for the power of God to "know the seed of God in one another"; (II) to be guided by God, to feel "a cross to your evil desires"; and (III) to receive that which "nourisheth up to everlasting life." In the third section, Fox cautions against, "the dreamer . . . and the lying spirit," which lead us into "that which is like the truth but is not the truth."

Note: Fox frequently uses "seed" as a metaphor for the inward Christ. Seed appears in phrases like "the seed Christ," Christ is "the seed of the woman," (i.e., the offspring of Eve, who God promised would "bruise the heel" of the serpent, Genesis 3:15; Epistle 130). Christ is "the suffering seed" (Epistle 101) and "the universal seed of God, which never sinned" (Epistle 251). Fox addresses Epistle 239 to "my dear friends and brethren, who are of the royal seed of God!" where being "royal seed" means being part of the family of God—those who received Christ were empowered to become children of God (John 1:12).

Scripture

In my Father's house are many dwelling places: if it were not
so, I would have tolde you: I go to prepare a place for you.
John 14:2 (GNV)

Hereby know we that we dwell in him, and he in
us, because he hath given us of his Spirit.
1 John 4:13 (KJV)

And the great dragon was cast out, that old serpent, called
the Devil, and Satan, which deceiveth the whole world.
Revelation 12:9 (KJV)

Epistle

All Friends,—

[I]

Dwell in that which is pure,
and wait for the power of God
to preserve you in that which is pure,
up to God.

And know the seed of God in one another,
that the knowledge which is after the flesh may die;
and know the power of God in one another.

Let your faith stand in that
which throws out the earthly nature,
and the loftiness of man;

which overturns the worldly wisdom
and the carnal knowledge,
which is brutish and devilish.

[II]

Dwell in that which is pure,
that ye may be able to discern,
and savour, and comprehend
that which is not pure;

and wait in that which is pure,
to have your minds guided thereby,
which will let you see God,

and show you your evil thoughts,
and judge them; and is a cross
to your evil desires, wills, and lusts.

[III]

I say, dwell in that which is pure,
which will guide you to God;
but if ye lust, . . . then the pure is veiled,

and the light mind speaks at random,
with a drunken spirit,
and not from the mouth of the Lord.

And there lodgeth the dreamer,
and the lying spirit, and the false prophet,
and that which is like the truth but is not the truth;

but dwelling in the truth,
this will be discovered.

And wait upon God in that which is pure,
for the receiving of that which comes from God,
which is living, which nourisheth up
to everlasting life.

So God Almighty be with you!

The Cross Overturns the World in the Heart (Epistle 51, 1653)

Introductory Note

The 1650s were a time of religious and class civil war in England. The Puritan-dominated Parliament sought to establish a government based in biblical values and where power would rest in (some of) the people rather than the monarchy. Many Friends came from the ranks of Cromwell's army, which had recently defeated the army of the monarchy. Disillusioned that political change was not profound enough, they gladly received Fox's call to exchange war with outward weapons for the war of the Lamb, fought with spiritual weapons (as in Epistle 55). Among these former soldiers was James Nayler, who was for a while, the foremost Quaker preacher, until he discredited Friends by allowing his exuberant followers to set him on a donkey and reenact Jesus' triumphal entry. To all who would overturn the oppressive powers of the world, Fox has a word of advice: see that the world is overturned in you first.

This excerpt begins, "The cross is to the carnal part, which is the ground of images." In the KJV, the word "images" almost always refers to idols—humanly invented gods and ideology. The Book of Revelation contrasts the Beast and the Lamb. The Beast depends on economic and military power: "As many as would not worship the image of the beast should be killed" (Rev 13:15, KJV). The Lamb, by contrast, is meek and is described as "slain from the foundation of the world" (Rev 13:8, KJV). The Lamb's way is the way of the cross. "Which cross," says Fox, "must be taken up by all. . . ." By this, Fox means an inward and spiritual practice of renouncing self-will "and all the evil things of the world." One of those things to be renounced is the myth that physical violence against those perceived to be "evil-doers" is redemptive and ennobles the warrior.

Fox titled this epistle, *To Friends, concerning the cross of Christ, the power of God, that leads out of the world, to the world that is without end.*

Scripture

And he said to them all, If any man will come after me, let him deny himself, and take up his cross daily, and follow me.
Luke 9:23 (KJV)

Love not the world, neither the things that are in the world. If any man love the world, the love of the Father is not in him.
1 John 2:15 (KJV)

And the gates of it [the New Jerusalem] shall not be shut at all by day: for there shall be no night there. . . . And there shall in no wise enter into it any thing that defileth.
Revelation 21:25, 27 (KJV)

Epistle

The cross is to the carnal part,
which is the ground of images,
the ground of the seducers,
and the ground of the false prophet
        and antichrist;

the cross is to that ground,
the root and life of it.

This being minded,
which is pure and eternal,
it makes a separation from
all other lovers,
        and brings to God,

and the ground of evil thoughts
comes to be opened,
and the cross is to that ground;
which cross overturns the world
        in the heart.

Which cross must be taken up
by all, who follow Jesus Christ
out of the world which hath an end,
into the world which is without end;

and all the evil things of the world
        must be denied.

For "who loves the world,
the love of the Father is not in him";
but where the world is standing,
the cross is not lived in.

But dwelling in the cross to the world,
here the love of God is shed abroad in the heart,

and the way is opened
into the inheritance which fades not away;
where nothing shall enter which is defiled. . . .

Therefore,
all in your measure, which is of God, wait,
that it may guide your minds up to God,
        and follow it,

and not your evil desires, nor the lust of the world;
for the fear of the Lord will keep your hearts clean,
and the true wisdom will be with you
        in the pure heart. . . .

Royal Seed: Royal Law (Epistle 74, 1654)

Introductory Note

Living in the "Royal Seed" (Jesus) necessarily results in a transformed life. Three marks of that life are: (1) "love enemies"; (2) equality—"to respect men's persons is a transgression of the royal law"; and (3) sexual purity—having but one spouse, "the bed of purity. . . ." These three "testimonies" don't always fit well in the liberal/conservative divide of today's culture wars, but for Fox, they are hallmarks of the counter-cultural way of the children of Light. Are there underlying principles here that are relevant in our culture?

Note that in the poem that concludes this excerpt, Fox's reference to "virgins pure" includes all the faithful, regardless of gender. To "respect men's persons" means to improperly show partiality for someone (see the OED); Fox usually applies it to class distinctions.

Scripture

If ye fulfil the royal law according to the scripture, Thou shalt love thy neighbour as thyself, ye do well: But if ye have respect to persons, ye commit sin, and are convinced of the law as transgressors. For whosoever shall keep the whole law, and yet offend in one *point*, he is guilty of all. For he that said, Do not commit adultery, said also, Do not kill. Now if thou commit no adultery, yet if thou kill, thou art become a transgressor of the law.
James 2:8–11 (KJV)

Then shall the kingdom of heaven be likened unto ten virgins, which took their lamps, and went forth to meet the bridegroom. And five of them were wise, and five *were* foolish. They that *were* foolish took their lamps, and took no oil with them: But the wise took oil in their vessels with their lamps. While the bridegroom tarried, they all slumbered and slept. And at midnight there was a cry made, Behold, the bridegroom cometh; go ye out to meet him. Then all those virgins arose, and trimmed their lamps.
Matthew 25:1–7 (KJV)

Epistle

My dear friends,—live in the immortal seed and power of the Lord God, that ye may meet in that, and in that feel one another. And live in the spirit, in which ye will have unity and peace. . . . And dwell in the peaceable seed, which destroyeth that which causeth troubles, wars, and fightings. . . .

And the everlasting command of the royal seed is, to love enemies, . . . for ye are all brethren, not ruling in lordship, like Jews and Gentiles, but the greatest shall be as the least among you; for the seed is one in all, and that is the master, who destroyeth the devil.

And to respect men's persons is a transgression of the royal law; let there be no such thing among you. But let every one believe in the light, and then in it see their salvation; and ye will receive power to become the sons of God.

Let no one have but one wife, for Christ hath but one, his church, which is his people.

So in the power and in the bed of purity,
in the singleness of virginity,
and in the beauty of holiness live,

where righteousness, and holiness, and truth dwell together,
and peace in the kingdom of power,
where is the everlasting joy, peace, and dominion, and victory,

where the bed is not defiled,
but the marriage that is honourable is known;
in that live.

About am I compassed with the virgins pure,
and the undefiled ones are my joy.
The virgins trimmed with oil in their lamps,
enter in with the bridegroom.

And all ye virgins pure,
lose not the ornaments of the Lord,
but wait,

that ye may be married to the lamb
in the everlasting marriage,
and remain with him
in the world that is without end.

The Unchangeable Life (Epistle 76, 1654)

Introductory Note

Fox, writing in a time of upheaval and civil war, warns us that a culture of change is like a churning ocean "by which dirt is cast up" and calls us to live "in the unchangeable life and power, and seed of God." We also live in a time of profound change. How do we discern "continuing revelation" that reflects God's liberating power from cultural change which draws us away from God? Can we assert the dependability of Truth in a post-modern era?

Note: there is a potential source of confusion with two very different meanings of the word "low" in this extract. Fox begins by warning, "be out of the low, earthly, changeable spirit of the world," but later, he says, "be wise and low, and take heed of abusing the power of God." The first "low" means degraded; the second "low" means humble or meek (OED).

Scripture

And, Thou, Lord, in the beginning hast laid the foundation of the earth; and the heavens are the works of thine hands: They shall perish; but thou remainest; and they all shall wax old as doth a garment; And as a vesture shalt thou fold them up, and they shall be changed: but thou art the same, and thy years shall not fail.

Hebrews 1:10–12 (KJV)

Epistle

O all Friends!
in the unchangeable life and power, and seed of God live,
and be out of the low, earthly, changeable spirit of the world,
which is given to changing and tossing,
and tempest and waves, by which dirt is cast up.

Oh! therefore, . . .
stand steadfast in the unchangeable life and seed of God,
which was before changings and alterings were;
and which will remain when they all are gone.

So, God Almighty in that preserve you,
in which ye may have the blessing among you,
and God's wisdom to order you, both men and women,
to his glory;

that so in his fear ye may be preserved
to the glory of God, in his wisdom and life,
in that which doth not change,
in which ye may feel the unchangeable fellowship.

And friends, be wise and low,
and take heed of abusing the power of God;
but live in it, in the still life, patient,
to the answering the good in all.

The Love which Does Not Change (Epistle 77, 1654)

Introductory Note

When we come to the unchangeable love and purity of God, that which is changeable in us must be removed. This is the work of the Spirit. Our faith is not in outward teaching, or doctrinal affirmations, but in God's love operating inwardly on a level deeper than the intellect.

The admonition, "keep your meetings, and ye will feel the seed of God among you all, though never a word be spoken," reflects a wonderful confidence in the living presence of God and in the human capacity to feel God's love expressed deep in the soul.

Scripture

The LORD hath appeared of old unto me, *saying*, Yea,
I have loved thee with an everlasting love: therefore
with lovingkindness have I drawn thee.
Jeremiah 31:3 (KJV)

Epistle

Friends, in the measure of the life of God wait,
to guide your minds up to the Father of life,
where there is no shadow nor changing.

As ye come hither,
ye must know a removing
and changing of that which will change,
with that which doth not change . . .

So here the love of God will come
to be shed abroad in your hearts,
which love is one,
and doth not change;

in it dwell, . . .

that over all that which is contrary to the Lord of life, . . . ye may reign every one over your own hearts, and lusts, and vile affections, and your former vile conversation, disposition, and nature, and wills. . . .

And, my dear friends, keep your meetings,
and ye will feel the seed of God among you all,
though never a word be spoken among you.

But be faithful,
that ye may answer that of God in every one.
And do not neglect your talents. . . .

Concerning the Light (Epistle 105, 1655)

Introductory Note

I have divided this epistle into four sections: (I) Jesus Christ is the source of the Light; (II) the reign of Christ has come and the power of the serpent ended; (III) waiting in the covenant of Light brings us to the beginning, before darkness was; (IV) waiting in the Light, we receive—in the heart—the word, which is the power for ministry. It is "the same word" that inspired the scriptures. Fox instructed that this epistle was "to be read amongst Friends," which suggests that these messages were read aloud in gatherings of Friends—an extension of Fox's spoken ministry.

Fox titled two epistles, *Concerning the Light*. The second, Epistle 155, has been renamed, "In the Light Rejoicing."

Scripture

In him was life; and the life was the light of men. . . . *That* was the true Light, which lighteth every man that cometh into the world.
John 1:4, 9 (KJV)

The word is nigh thee, *even* in thy mouth, and in thy heart: that is, the word of faith, which we preach.
Romans 10:8 (KJV)

[God] hath saved us, and called us with an holy calling, not according to our works, but according to his own purpose and grace, which was given us in Christ Jesus before the world began.
2 Timothy 1:9 (KJV)

Epistle

[I]

All Friends every where, keep your meetings
waiting in the light
which comes from the Lord Jesus Christ;
so will ye receive power from him,

and have the refreshing springs of life
opened to your souls, and be kept sensible
of the tender mercies of the Lord.

And know one another in the life,
(ye that be turned to the light,)
and in the power which comes
from the Lord Jesus Christ,
who is your light,
who is your life;

that ye may all in the life
see Christ to reign in you,
who is the truth,
from whence ye have light.

[II]

Here the old serpent is chained,
and put into the bottomless pit,
and Christ is known to reign,
and ye to reign with him;

heirs with him, joint-heirs,
and heirs of God.

Here is the dominion
received and witnessed
of the world that is without end,

and the promise of life
from the Father of life
to you, who are turned to the son,
who to the Father is the way,
who is the mediator
between the Father and you.

[III]

All wait to receive the everlasting priest,
the everlasting covenant of God,
of light, life, and peace;
into which covenant no sin,
no darkness, nor death comes. . . .

But ye that are turned to the light
walk in the light,
walk in the truth,
where no darkness is;

with which light, that never changeth,
ye may come to see that which was in the beginning,
before the world was,
where there is no shadow nor darkness.

[IV]

In which light as ye wait,
ye will come to receive into your hearts
the word of faith,
which reconciles to God,

and is as a hammer,
to beat down all that is contrary;
and as a sword,
to divide the precious from the vile;
and as a fire,
to burn up that which is contrary to the precious:

which word is pure, and endureth for ever;
which was in the beginning,
and is now again witnessed and made manifest.

Therefore wait in the light,
that ye may all receive it,
the same word that ever was,
which the scriptures were given forth from. . . .

A Christology of the Light (Epistle 130, 1656)

Introductory Note

Originally, this is part of a much longer work titled, *To all Friends, to dwell in the truth, the life of God, the light, &c.* These excerpts begin with Fox asserting the identity of Jesus ("born of a virgin, crucified, and is ascended") with the cosmic Christ ("the power of God . . . by whom the world was made"). At the end, Fox brings us back to Jesus with the lovely expression, "the seed, which the grave could not hold under."

Christ is the "savior within" and our "mediator" with God. Christ is "the seed of the woman" (Eve) who must "bruise the serpent's head in every one of you" (see Genesis 3:15, KJV). Christ is "the light of the world" (John 8:12, KJV) who "doth enlighten every man that cometh into the world" (John 1:9, KJV). Christ is "the power of God" in which we must "dwell." Christ is "the bread of life," the source of eternal life. The power of God is "the cross of Christ . . . and there is no other." (See Epistle 51 for Fox on the inner work of the cross in believers.)

If the cascade of metaphors in this epistle becomes confusing, the core is simple. There is a new life of righteousness available to all. This is through Christ, Emmanuel, God with us—known within by those who "wait to find him, and receive him." As we dwell in the light, and "be low, as babes and little children," Christ becomes "master." Our passions and lusts (which used to have mastery) are supplanted by "the wisdom of God." Fox's counsel is, "let the seed be master in the male and in the female." We come to be the agents of God's wisdom in ordering the world. In this, the power of God is manifested in and among us.

Scripture

All things were made by him; and without him was not any thing
made that was made. In him was life; and the life was the light of men.
John 1:3–4 (KJV)

For by him were all things created, that are in heaven, and that are in
earth, visible and invisible, whether *they be* thrones, or dominions,
or principalities, or powers: all things were created by him, and for
him: And he is before all things, and by him all things consist.
Colossians 1:16–17 (KJV)

For the preaching of the cross is to them that perish foolishness;
but unto us which are saved it is the power of God.
1 Corinthians 1:18 (KJV)

And if Christ *be* in you, the body *is* dead because of
sin; but the Spirit *is* life because of righteousness.
Romans 8:10 (KJV)

And I will put enmity between thee and the woman,
and between thy seed and her seed; it shall bruise
thy head, and thou shalt bruise his heel.
Genesis 3:15 (KJV)

Epistle

All Friends, . . . this is the word of the Lord God, and a charge to you all in the presence of the Lord God, heed the power and life, the power which ye have formerly known and tasted of. . . .

> For Christ is the power of God,
> to whom the angels must bow.
>
> And Christ Jesus,
> who was born of a virgin,
> crucified, and is ascended,
> and there is no other,
>
> all of you, that are turned to the light,
> wait to have him born in you,
> every one in particular.
>
> "I am the light of the world," saith Christ,
> by whom the world was made,
> who doth enlighten "every man, that cometh into the world."
>
> Who is the "bread of life,
> that came down from above;
> and who eateth of this bread, lives for ever."

Now, every one of you having a light from Christ, the bread of life, wait, and with and from it you will see, know, and have your food in due season. . . .

> And who go from the light within,
> go from the Emmanuel,
> from the saviour within, Christ Jesus,
>
> and from the truth in the inward parts,
> and from the mediator between you and God,
> and from the vine;
> and so, ye bear not fruit to the glory of God.

And going from the light within,
ye go from your peace,
and from the covenant of God;

and going from the light within,
ye go from the life,
where every one receives the light of life.

And who go from the light within,
        go from the increase of God;
who go from the light within,
        go from the anointing within them,
and so continue not in the son, nor in the Father.

All who go from the light within,
go out of the covenant of eternal life.

But every one walking in the light within,
        which he hath received,
        he shall there receive the bread of life,
Christ, whom the light comes from. . . .

So every particular of you,
to you this is the word of the Lord God,
know the son of God to be revealed in you.

And know the seed, which is Christ,
to which the promise of God is;
that ye may all witness the seed of the woman
to bruise the serpent's head in every one of you.

That you may all witness
ye are come to him that was in the beginning;
and to the seed of the woman,
which bruiseth the serpent's head
in every one of you in your own particulars.

Then ye all will come to feed on the bread of life, that comes from above. . . .

And this is the counsel of the Lord God to you,
dwell all in the power of God,
which is the gospel of peace.

And the power of God is the cross of Christ;
and ye that feel the power of God, ye feel Christ;
for Christ is the power of God.

The power of God is but one,
and the light is but one,
and the cross of Christ is but one,
which is the power of God;

and the gospel of truth is but one,
which is the power of God,
and there is no other.

Ye that come to know these,
look for no other.

And Christ is that one in the male and in the female,
which is the seed,
which the promise of God is to;
and there all wait to find him,
and receive him.

"Know ye not, that Christ Jesus is in you, except ye are reprobates," said the apostle. . . .

And if Christ Jesus be in you,
the body of sin is dead,
and ye are brought to God;

and the Emmanuel being known,
"God with us" is witnessed
by every one of you, that are redeemed by him
out of the transgression,
who are in the second Adam.

So, if Christ Jesus be in you, and ye in him,
          the body is dead;
and ye are alive to righteousness,
and death is brought into death.

Friends, dwell all in the light, and then ye will dwell in covenant with God, and with God ye will have peace.

And friends,
all dwell in the light,
that ye may receive the wisdom of God,

by which all things were created;
with which wisdom
ye may come to order all the creatures.

And be low,
as babes and little children,
for the little children receive the kingdom.

And so,
all know the promise which is to the seed;
and know the seed of God in one another,

that there be no master but Christ,
who bruiseth the serpent's head,
          where debate and enmity are,
          which are the cause of strife.

So, let the seed be master
in the male and in the female,
          that the ground of strife,
          which would be master,
          may be kept under,

and the seed,
which the grave could not hold under,
be the ruler. . . .

Own the Light (Epistle 139, 1657)

Introductory Note

The essence of the Quaker message and spiritual practice was the reality and power of the light within. In this epistle, Fox repeatedly uses the phrase, "owns the light," which, in this context, means to confess to be true or valid (OED). This is crucial, for ultimately, it is the Light which comes from Christ that leads us into relationship with God.

Note the connection Fox makes between "dwelling in the light" and "praying in the Spirit" with having "the spirit . . . to guide them." For Fox, living according to the guidance of the Spirit is the way out of "the wrath," "out of wars," and even "out of the occasion of wars."

Scripture

> Likewise the Spirit also helpeth our infirmities: for we know not what we should pray for as we ought: but the Spirit itself maketh intercession for us with groanings which cannot be uttered.
> Romans 8:26 (KJV)

Epistle

Friends,—

Know the praying in the spirit,
and with the understanding;
then ye will come to know the sighs and groans
that cannot be uttered.

For such as have not the spirit . . . to guide them,
are as the Pharisees were,
    in the long prayers,
    and in the wrath,
    and in the doubting,
    and do not lift up holy hands. . . .

And none owns the light as it is [in] Jesus,
but he that owns the light
that Christ lighteth him withal.

And none owns the truth,
but who owns the light
that cometh from Christ, the truth.

And none cometh to the Father,
but such who owns the light
that cometh from Christ, which leads to him.

Nor none owns the son,
except he owns the light
that cometh from him.

For all dwelling in the light that comes from Jesus,

it leads out of wars,
leads out of strife,
leads out of the occasion of wars,
and leads out of the earth up to God,
out of earthly-mindedness to heavenly-mindedness,

and bringeth your minds
to be in heaven.

Be Low and Still (Epistle 146, 1657)

Introductory Note

This epistle is addressed *To Friends in Ireland* and comes about eight years after Cromwell's campaign to subdue Ireland in which he caused some three thousand to be slaughtered at Drogheda and another two thousand at Wexford (Healey:274). Fox calls Friends to "be low and still" and thus "answer that of God in every one, that crieth for peace and rest." This is the full text of the epistle.

Scripture

That your faith should not stand in the wisdom
of men, but in the power of God.
1 Corinthians 2:5 (KJV)

Epistle

Friends,—

Feel all of you the power of the Lord God
in yourselves to guide your minds up to God,
and to give you dominion over all weakness,
and to strengthen and to heal you.

And look not out, but every one
feel the power of God in your own particulars,
and let all your faith stand in that;

then will ye have unity,
and in that ye will have dominion and victory,
and it will keep you in order.

In which ye will have virtue,
and in which ye will feel the spirit,
in which ye will have fellowship and comfort.

And be low and still in the life and power,
and not hasty nor rash;
that ye may, in the life and power,
answer that of God in every one
that crieth for peace and rest.

So dwell in the love of God,
(this I warn you and charge every one of you;)

your faith standing in this and in the power of God,
then ye will feel the presence of the Lord God
among you.

In the Light Rejoicing (Epistle 155, 1657)

Introductory Note

This was the second epistle Fox titled *Concerning the Light*, (the other being Epistle 105), so for clarity I have given this one a new title. It is one of the clearest statements of the everlasting gospel: in this life, we can be "partakers" of eternal life, when we dwell in the Light. Waiting in the Light, we receive power (1) to become the children of God and (2) to have a "witness" of the eternal in ourselves that reaches from the present to "the world which is to come."

Scripture

> But lay up treasures for your selves in heaven, where neither the mothe nor canker corrupteth, and where theeves neither digge through, nor steale.
> Matthew 6:20 (GNV)

> And there are three that bear witness in earth, the Spirit, and the water, and the blood: and these three agree in one. . . . And this is the record, that God hath given to us eternal life, and this life is in his Son. He that hath the Son hath life; *and* he that hath not the Son of God hath not life.
> 1 John 5:8, 11–12 (KJV)

Epistle

Friends,—

Ye that be turned to the light
in it wait,
in it meet together,
that with it your hearts may be joined together
up to Christ, the head,
from whence the light doth come . . .

[Y]e believing in the light and receiving it,
ye receive and come into the covenant with God,
and peace with God;
and into that which gives the knowledge
of his glory
and of his image.

And this belief giveth the victory over the world,
and brings unto God, and into his likeness,
and separates you from the world, and its likeness,
and image, and its fashion,
which are out of the light. . . .

But in the light rejoicing
and walking,
ye receive the love of God
shed abroad into your hearts . . .
and know God and his law put in your minds,
and in your hearts written. . . .

In this waiting, in the light,
the world where there is no end
it gives you to see;

and the power
of the world which is to come,
ye will come to see

and be partakers of.

Which power ye receiving (who are in the light,)
it brings you to become the sons of God,
and to be heirs of the world where there is no end,

and of the everlasting inheritance which fadeth not away,
and the riches which are durable,
where no thief can come,
nor nothing to rust or canker. . . .

Therefore walk in the light as the children of the light,
and know the wisdom that is of her children justified;
that ye may answer the light
in every one that comes into the world
that hateth it.

And keep your habitations,
that ye may every one feel your spring
in the light which comes from the Lord,

and feel your nourishment and refreshment;
which waters the plants
and causeth them to grow up in the Lord,
from whom the pure, living springs come.

And here is the water
which is the witness in the earth,
which doth wash;

and here comes the spirit to be known,
the witness which doth baptize,
and the witness, the blood, which doth cleanse,

which agrees with the witness in heaven.
So, he that believes hath the witness in himself.

(Mark and take notice.)

And so, ye being in the light,
(every one in particular)
feed upon the bread of life
which comes from above,
which nourisheth up to eternal life

wherein as every one grows up,
here every one gives glory
to the Father, and to the son,
and knows the light which is

the way, the truth, and the life.

Every one of you that are turned to it,
ye are in

the one way, truth, light, and life,

feeding upon the one bread which comes from above;
which whosoever doth eat of lives for ever,
and shall never die.

Let this be read among all Friends every where. . . . Let no Friends be discouraged; but walk in the truth and the love of it, and to it bend.

Sing and Pray in the Spirit (Epistle 167, 1658)

Introductory Note

In the days of the Commonwealth, the established church was just Puritan, not Anglican. In 1658, Cromwell imposed a number of days of fasting and took up a nation-wide collection in support of Protestants in Europe (Ni:348–349). This epistle seems like Fox's response. There is no "life" in a government-serving church, but there is joyful freedom amongst those who no longer quench the Holy Spirit and who gladly join in the true fast that "lets the oppressed go free."

Scripture

What is it then? I will pray with the spirit, and I will pray with the understanding also: I will sing with the spirit, and I will sing with the understanding also.
1 Corinthians 14:15 (KJV)

Is not this the fast that I have chosen? to loose the bands of wickedness, to undo the heavy burdens, and to let the oppressed go free, and that ye break every yoke?
Isaiah 58:6 (KJV)

Epistle

My dear friends,—

Be not carried away by good words and fair speeches . . . but every one have hold of the truth in yourselves, and the life, and light, and power of the Most High, by which ye may be stayed upon Christ, your bread of life; he is the staff of your heavenly and eternal life. . . .

Now friends,

who have denied the world's songs and singing;
sing ye in the spirit, and with grace,
making melody in your hearts to the Lord.

And ye having denied the world's formal praying,
pray ye always in the spirit, and watch in it.

And ye that have denied the world's giving of thanks,
and their saying of grace, and living out of it;
do ye in every thing give thanks to the Lord
through Jesus Christ.

And ye that have denied the world's praising God with their lips,

whilst their hearts are afar off;
do ye always praise the Lord night and day,
and from the rising of the sun
to the going down of the same, praise ye the Lord.

And ye that have denied the world's fastings,
and of their hanging down their heads like a bulrush for a day,
who smite with the fist of wickedness,

keep ye the fast of the Lord
that breaks the bond of iniquity,
and lets the oppressed go free;

that your health may grow,
and your light may shine
as the morning.

As a Pleasant Field (Epistle 183, 1659)

Introductory Note

Fox shows us a safe place where we may be refreshed and healed from the turmoils and traumas of our daily lives.

Note that this lovely blessing is given in the interest of a dynamic and tangible faith: the blessings (a) "may be felt." This is not an individual experience for (b) the blessings are felt "amongst you"—in a gathered community—and (c) they are felt amongst the community for a purpose, namely that, as a community, "ye may be all ordered" (governed) directly by God. Finally, this leads us to reach out (d) so that "ye do refresh others." This suggests a mode of evangelism based on sharing the experience of feeling blessed, rather than doctrine.

Scripture

And the LORD shall guide thee continually, and satisfy thy soul in drought, and make fat thy bones: and thou shalt be like a watered garden, and like a spring of water, whose waters fail not.
Isaiah 58:11 (KJV)

Epistle

Friends,—

Dwell in patience,
and in the power, life and wisdom of God,
and in peace and love and unity
one with another.

And be subject in the power,
and life and wisdom of God
to God and to one another;

that in it ye may be
as a pleasant field to the Lord God,

and as the lilies,
and the flowers,
and the buds,

feeling the pleasant showers
and the streams of life from the living God
flowing upon you
and coming into you,

whereby the presence and blessing
of the Lord God Almighty
amongst you all may be felt. . . .

And the God of all peace keep you,
that nothing may reign and rule amongst you

but the life,
and power, and seed,
and wisdom of God

that in him ye may be preserved
by which all things
were made and created.

That ye may be all ordered to his glory,
and be a good savour in the hearts of all people;
in which ye do refresh others
and are refreshed. . . .

Hear the Voice from Heaven that Shakes the Earth (Epistle 184, 1659)

Introductory Note

Fox contrasts the voice from heaven with the "chambers of imagery." God's voice is like an earthquake that breaks down everything that is not "eternal." The "chamber of imagery"—a phrase from the prophet Ezekiel, denoting a secret room with idols (images) and foreign conspiracies—is for Fox, everything we do in our own willfulness. The silence of Quaker worship is a valuable laboratory for learning to discern the voice that speaks from heaven, and to learn what needs to be shaken loose in us, and to distinguish true (heavenly) joy from false (worldly) joys.

Scripture

> See that ye refuse not him that speaketh. For if they escaped not who refused him that spake on earth, much more *shall not we escape*, if we turn away from him that *speaketh* from heaven: Whose voice then shook the earth: but now he hath

promised, saying, Yet once more I shake not the earth only, but also heaven. And this *word*, Yet once more, signifieth the removing of those things that are shaken, as of things that are made, that those things which cannot be shaken may remain.

Hebrews 12:25–28 (KJV)

Then said he unto me, Son of man, hast thou seen what the ancients of the house of Israel do in the dark, every man in the chambers of his imagery? for they say, The LORD seeth us not; the LORD hath forsaken the earth.

Ezekiel 8:12 (KJV)

Epistle

O my dear friends and brethren every where!

the power of the Lord God,
that is over all, live in,
that in that ye may feel unity and fellowship;

that in the power of the Lord God
ye may all come to be heirs
of the power of an endless life,
through which ye may inherit eternity,
and so to feel life eternal abiding in you. . . .

And so, all to live in that
which is the same to-day, as was yesterday,
Christ Jesus, the power of God,
and the seed of life,
and word that was in the beginning. . . .

So, hear his voice every where,
that speaks from heaven,
whose voice shakes the earth,
and not the earth only, but heaven also.

The heaven signifies joy;
 so, all the false joys,
 the lifted up joys,
 or exalted joy,
 and joy in vain glory,
 and joy in the world,
 or any outward thing or creature,
 or men or women,

his voice, that speaks from heaven,
shakes the earth and the heavens,
and these must be shaken and removed,
both the heaven and the earth,
before that doth appear that can never be shaken. . . .

And there is the true joy, the standing joy,
in that which is from everlasting to everlasting,
who is the beginning and ending;
here is not any lifted up, nor cast down.

So I say, hear his voice,
and harden not your hearts;
for through not hearing his voice,
ye harden your hearts,
then ye provoke God to wrath and sore displeasure.

Let him have your ear,
that speaks from heaven;
that ye may come to observe his counsel,
teachings, instructions, and directions. . . .

And as your ears are attentive
to the Lord's voice that is from heaven,
iniquity's mouth is stopped in you,
the throne of iniquity is thrown down in you,
that is, the wicked spirit and power, wherein iniquity sits,
and the chamber of imagery is thrown down in you,
where man's thoughts and imaginations are.

But as the ear is attentive to the voice of him
that speaks from heaven,
ye will come to the throne of the Lamb,
who hath the victory and the dominion;
that all may live in the everlasting power of God. . . .

Perfection (Epistle 262, 1668)

Introductory Note

Fox opens with a ruthless condemnation of anything that "has led you from God." The shocking language of execution reflects Fox's belief that toleration of wrong leads to persistence in wrong-doing. Whatever is "condemned by the light" must be completely renounced. It is essential that this word of admonition is followed, immediately, by a picture of God's love and mercy. Perfection starts from within—not from following rules. Fox echoes Paul in saying it is "Christ in you" who "makes perfect," and he draws on the new covenant promise to call "every man and woman" to "truth in the inward parts." What is perfection? It is being "led by the spirit of God" and thus becoming a child of God. This doctrine of genuine perfection in this world through the presence of "Christ in you" (the Light within) is set in contrast to doctrines that insist that people cannot be truly good in their lifetimes, which Fox describes as crying up a "body of sin and death on this side of the grave, with their hypocrite's hope" (for the Protestants), and "purgatory" (for the Catholics).

Scripture

For the law made nothing perfect, but the bringing in of a
better hope *did*; by the which we draw nigh unto God.
Hebrews 7:19 (KJV)

To them God has chosen to make known among the Gentiles the glorious riches of this mystery, which is Christ in you, the hope of

glory. We proclaim him, admonishing and teaching everyone with all wisdom, so that we may present everyone perfect in Christ.
Colossians 1:27–28 (NIV)

Behold, thou desirest truth in the inward parts: and in the hidden *part* thou shalt make me to know wisdom.
Psalm 51:6 (KJV)

I will put my law in their inward parts, and write it in their hearts.
Jeremiah 31:33 (KJV)

Epistle

[Part I: Condemned by the Light.]

All Friends and people,

that is to be condemned in yourselves,
which hath led you
from Christ,
from God,
and from unity in the light;

I say,
that is condemned by the light,
and must be executed and killed,
and stoned with the living stone,
and run through with the living sword,
and hammered down with the living hammer to pieces,
and burnt up with the living fire,
and so made an end of.

For that which leads into looseness,
whimsies, imaginations, false visions,
though it be condemned,

yet,
if it be not executed,
it is in danger to rise again;

and if it rise again,
and get over you,
it will be your ruler,
if it get out of prison and be alive . . .

If a child be fallen down into the dirt, [the child's father] doth not go and tumble him more into the dirt, or into the ditch, and there let him lie in the dirt and ditch, but takes him out and washes him; and so doth the heavenly Father, who leads his children by his hand, and dandles them upon his knee. And so, all that be called fathers in the truth, or mothers, their tenderness should be the same to all little children in the truth, . . . that sometimes may fall into the dirt and ditch, and slip aside, and then be troubled, and cry. To such there should be tenderness shown. . . .

For Christ is manifest in the flesh, to condemn sin in the flesh, . . . and makes an end of sin. . . . But the sin being condemned in the flesh, Christ is manifest in the flesh, so that they become Christ's. . . .

And these know the new life,
    which God is served in;
and these know the new earth,
    wherein dwells righteousness;
and these know the old earth,
    wherein dwell[s] unrighteousness.

And these can bring forth things new and old.
For they that are led by the spirit of God,
    are the sons of God. . . .

[Part II: Christ In You, the Hope of Glory.]

The true hope,
the true cross,
the true faith,
the true worship,

the true religion,
the true way,
true image,
and true fellowship

have been lost since the apostles' days,
amongst those called christians,
who are out of the life.

And they that have lost the cross of Christ, which is the power of God, . . . have set up a purgatory to cleanse them when they are dead. And others cry up a body of sin and death on this side of the grave, with their hypocrite's hope; and they have lost the true ministry, and set up a false one, to preach up imperfection. . . .

And people were imperfect in old Adam
before Christ came;
for the law made nothing perfect;

but the true minister,
Christ in you the hope of glory,
doth make perfect,
both in the apostles' days and now.

"Christ in you, the hope of glory," said the apostle,
"whom we preach, warning every man,
that we may present every man
perfect in Christ Jesus."

So the perfection is in Christ Jesus;
the imperfection is in old Adam.

So this is the true hope
that purifies,
which every one that hath it
purifies himself,
even as he is pure. . . .

And the true faith hath been lost since the apostles' days;

> the true faith which purifies the heart,
> which is the faith of God's elect,
> which faith gives victory
> over that which separates from God;
>
> in which faith ye all please God;
> which faith is the gift of God,
> and Christ is the author of it:
>
> every one look unto him for it,
> for the finishing of it,
> who is the author of it. . . .

And all that are out of this faith, they cry no victory while we are upon the earth . . . ; these . . . cannot preach the true and living faith of God's elect. . . . "The life that I now live, is by the faith of the son of God; yet it is not I, but Christ that lives in me," said the apostle. . . .

> And the true worship hath been lost
> since the apostles' days;
> yea, the worship that Christ set up
> above sixteen hundred years since,
>
> in the spirit and in the truth;
> yea, in the spirit of God,
> which was before the spirit of the devil was,. . . .
>
> and so every man and woman
> must come to truth in the inward parts,
> and to the spirit of God
> within themselves,
>
> > if they be worshippers of God
> > in the spirit and truth,
> > which the devil abode not in.

And this is the standing and perfect worship,
in which there is unity in the truth;
for the enmity is out of it,
and he cannot get into it.

Glory be to God for ever!. . . .

And the true way is lost since the apostles' days, which Christ set up above sixteen hundred years since; who said, 'I am the way to the Father; and no man cometh to the Father, but by me.'

So no one comes out of old Adam,
but by Christ, the second Adam.
No one comes out of darkness,
but by Christ, the light;

no one comes out of death,
and from under the prince of death,
        the power of it,
but by Christ, the life.
So he is the way to God.

No one comes out of unrighteousness,
but by Christ, the righteousness;
no one comes out of the wisdom below,
but by Christ, who is the wisdom of God,
which is from above. . . .

And none come to this new and living way,
        Christ Jesus,
        but who come to
the grace of God in their hearts;
the spirit of God in their hearts.

So he is the new and the living way,
who is the first and the last,
the beginning and the ending,
set up from everlasting to everlasting. . . .

And the true religion hath been lost, and erred from, since the apostles' days.

The religion that is pure from above,
and undefiled before God,
which keeps from the spots of the world,
which is to visit the widows and the fatherless.

Now they that are out of this religion
have made many religions,
but they are spotted and defiled. . . .

And their widows, and their fatherless,
    and strangers
go begging up and down
their streets and highways;

so their streets and highways
are judges against them. . . .

And the image of God in them hath been lost since the apostles' days, that man and woman were renewed into by Christ. . . . But now is Christ renewing man again into the image of God. . . .

Glory to God for ever,
for his image and his likeness
is led into by Christ Jesus,

and into Adam and Eve's state before they fell;
and not only into that state,
but into Christ Jesus that never fell.

And the true praying hath been lost since the apostles' days; for none can pray truly, but by the spirit of God. . . . And all they that have erred from the spirit . . . make prayers, and say them over, and give them to others to say over; and so pray by the book; . . . and so . . . grieve, and vex, and quench the spirit of God. . . . And every one must come to the spirit of God in themselves, and to the light. . . .

And the true fellowship hath been lost . . . since the apostles' days. . . .

Now the gospel fellowship is a perfect fellowship,
a pure and a holy fellowship,
it is an everlasting fellowship;
for the power of God is everlasting. . . .

And they that say revelations are ceased,
they may as well say, there is no gospel;
and so have no Christ to preach. . . .

And the sanctifying belief hath been lost since the apostles' days;

for he that believes is born of God;
and he that believes in the light,
may become a child of the light;

every one that cometh into the world
are enlightened by Christ,
that they should believe in the light. . . .

For he that believes, overcomes the world;
for "greater is he that is in you,
than he that is in the world". . . .

Christ Has Enlightened Every Person (Epistle 388, 1683)

Introductory Note

This remarkable epistle, *To Friends that are captives at Algiers*, is dated *Gousey in Essex, the 10 th of the 2 nd month*, 1683. Groups of Friends had been taken prisoner in Mequinez, Morocco, and Algiers by pirates of the Barbary Coast. Fox had joined a delegation to see the Ambassador of Morocco on their behalf in 1682 (Ni:737). Addressing Friends held in "slavery and captivity," Fox urges them, first, to be humble to receive Christ's teaching and, second, to be bold in preaching the gospel with their "lives and words." Fox sees no conflict between humility and doctrinal clarity.

The epistle is remarkable for its clear statement of the universal Light of Christ and for the new covenant promise that the Spirit is for all people: "men and women, . . . whites and blacks, Moors, and Turks, and Indians, Christians, Jews, and Gentiles."

Note: in the second to last paragraph, the quoted words are a loose rendition of a passage from the Nicene Creed.

Scripture

For the grace of God has appeared, bringing salvation to all,
training us to renounce impiety and worldly passions, and in the
present age to live lives that are self-controlled, upright, and godly.
Titus 2:11–12 (NRS)

And you will be hated by all because of my name. But
the one who endures to the end will be saved.
Matthew 10:22 (NRS)

Epistle

Dear friends, who are captives in Algiers, whom the Lord hath enlightened with his day spring from on high, and visited you with his tender mercies in your slavery and captivity, . . . my desires are, that you may all keep low in humility, . . . for God dwells with the humble, and teaches the humble the way they should walk.

And therefore be careful of God's glory,
you who profess the name of God, and his son,
that your lives, and words, and conversations
may preach godliness, righteousness, holiness,
virtue, sobriety, and modesty,
both to Turks, Moors, Jews, and to your patrons,
and to the families where you live;

for Christ hath enlightened every man that comes into the
world,
he hath enlightened the Turks, Jews, and Moors, with the
light,
(which is the life in him the word,)
that all in the light might know God and Christ;

and "the grace of God which brings salvation
hath appeared unto all men";
so to the Turks, Jews, and Moors,
yea, to all nations;

so that with the grace of God
they may be taught to deny
ungodliness and unrighteousness, . . .

and God, who made all,
pours out of his spirit
upon all men and women in the world,
in the days of his new covenant,
yea, upon whites and blacks,
Moors, and Turks, and Indians,
Christians, Jews, and Gentiles,

that all with the spirit of God,
might know God and the things of God,
and serve and worship him in his spirit and truth,
that he hath given them.

But they that do resist the truth,
and quench, and vex, and grieve,
and rebel against the spirit that God hath given them,
such are not like to serve and worship God
in his spirit and truth;

but he that endures to the end
in God's grace,
spirit, light, and truth,
shall be saved. . . .

Now there is a common saying among the Turks to the Christians, "Your crucified God," meaning Christ. Now this is their mistake; though God was in Christ reconciling the world to himself, . . . Christ did not die as he was God, but as man. "He was crucified and buried, and rose again the third day, and ascended, and is at the right hand of God"; this he did by the power of God, as he was man. So the Turks arc mistaken, to say, or to think, that the eternal God could be crucified or die. . . .

And, friends, it would be very well for you, if you could get the Turks and Moors' language, that you might be the more enabled to direct them to the grace and spirit of God in them. . . .

The Fellowship of the Children of Light

While ye have light, believe in the light,
that ye may be the children of light.
John 12:36 (KJV)

The Peacemaker Has Dominion (Epistle 9, 1652)

Introductory Note

Those who dwell in the Light are formed into a fellowship that, in many ways, is different from the world. Here, in one of Fox's earliest epistles, he celebrates the nonviolent power of the Lamb of God. This epistle was written two years following the execution of King Charles I in 1649 by a faction of radical Puritans. They seized power in the Rump Parliament (1648–1653), so called because it was comprised of those who remained after they expelled about a hundred royalist and moderate members. (Healey:251) Their rule is "that which is set up by the sword."

By claiming that the Peacemaker has dominion, is Fox suggesting that, in every encounter, the way of nonviolence will prevail? No. In fact, Fox knows that Jesus suffered, and his followers will, too, and so he counsels, "Let the waves break over your heads." Fox also knows that, whatever the outward circumstances might be, there is a spiritual kingdom that is "come and coming." It is come already in the fellowship of the children of Light, and it is in the process of coming as the Quaker movement moves from the north country of England, south and out to rest of the world; and "the Lamb shall have the victory" (Rev 17:14).

Fox uses the phrase, "a new and living way," which, in the Letter to the Hebrews, is used to describe the new covenant, of which Christ is the mediator (Heb 8:5; 9:15). Hebrews chapters 8 through 10 is an extended discussion of the new covenant, first promised to Jeremiah.

Note, in the closing stanzas, the now-obsolete word, "withal," is a form of "with," used when "with" is placed at the end of a phrase. "Who" refers back to "the lamb" who will overcome using the nonviolent weapons of the Spirit and speech.

Scripture

And take the helmet of salvation, and the sword
of the Spirit, which is the word of God.
Ephesians 6:17 (KJV)

The earth is the LORD's, and the fulness thereof;
the world, and they that dwell therein.
Psalm 24:1 (KJV)

Epistle

Friends,—

That which is set up by the sword,
is held up by the sword;

and that which is set up by spiritual weapons,
is held up by spiritual weapons,
and not by carnal weapons.

The peacemaker has Dominion
over the peace-breaker,
to calm him in the power of God.

And Friends, let the waves break over your heads.
There is rising a new and living way out of the north,
which makes the nations like waters.

Hurt not the vines, nor the oil,
nor such as know that "the earth is the Lord's,
and the fulness thereof."

The days of virtue, love and peace
are come and coming,
and the Lamb had and has the kings of the earth
to war withal and to fight withal,

who will overcome
with the sword of the spirit,
the word of his mouth,
for the Lamb shall have the victory.

Mind the Oneness (Epistle 46, 1653)

Introductory Note

Here Fox celebrates the unity of those who love the Light and walk in it. Friends have a phrase, "a gathered meeting," to refer to those times in worship when we sense God gathering us in oneness with our fellow worshipers and we in oneness with God. Here, we discover a unity that is not dependent upon uniform doctrine nor ethnic, racial, or cultural background nor of class or education. Here, "there is no confusion but pureness and oneness." It is in that unity that we "see the church of God." This unity is the spiritual foundation on which Friends depend when we try to make decisions by discerning "the sense of the meeting" as to God's will, instead of by compromise or vote.

Scripture

That they all may be one; as thou, Father, *art* in me, and I in thee, that they also may be one in us: that the world may believe that thou hast sent me. And the glory which thou gavest me I have given them; that they may be one, even as we are one: I in them, and thou in me, that they may be made perfect in one; and that the world may know that thou hast sent me, and hast loved them, as thou hast loved me.

John 17:21–23 (KJV)

Epistle

To all Friends who are in the unity,
 which is in the light;
 walk in the light.
It is one light that doth convince you all;
and one Christ, that doth call all to repentance,
 up to himself
 the one head,
 which is Christ. . . .

Ye have all
one eye, which is the light;
one fire, which consumes
 all which the light discovers to be evil;
and one spirit, which baptizes all
 into the one body,
 where there is no confusion,
 but pureness and oneness.

Therefore all Friends,
mind the oneness;
and this one light
 leads you out of darkness
 into the everlasting day,

where ye see the church of God. . . .

[W]ho love the light,
and walk in the light,
Jesus Christ is their king,
 whose gospel is preached
 to every creature. . . .

Though the Way of Others Seems Diverse (Epistle 47, 1653)

Introductory Note

In this epistle, Fox calls for an open heart to the diversity of ways God may be moving in others, lest we "judge the Lord." "Imitation" and conformity will not get us anywhere spiritually. Instead, we are to walk with God with authenticity and "joy and peace." The humility to recognize that we are given a "measure of that Spirit," not "all of God," is a necessary starting point if we are to find the unity in that diverse community of those who dwell in the Light.

Scripture

But unto every one of us is given grace according
to the measure of the gift of Christ.
Ephesians 4:7 (KJV)

Epistle

All Friends every where— . . .

in the light dwell,
that ye may come to learn of Christ in the life,
and with it know the movings
of the spirit of life in you. . . .

A measure of this living spirit and power being known in every one, . . . therefore

every one of you know a measure of that spirit,
which exerciseth meekness, truth, and faithfulness
in you in power, . . .

that ye may all know, what it is to follow the Lamb
with joy and peace in your minds,
your hearts upright to your guide.

Take heed that none of you walk by imitation of others only. For though the way they walk in be good to them who are in the light, yet thou art in darkness, and knowest not whither thou goest. . . .

And take heed of judging the measures of others. . . .

And this know,

that there are diversities of gifts,
but one spirit, and unity therein
to all who with it are guided.

And though the way seems to thee diverse;
yet judge not the way,
lest thou judge the Lord,

and knowest not that several ways (seeming to reason) hath God to bring his people out by;

Deep is the mystery of godliness!
Therefore silence all flesh,
and see your own ways be clean. . . .

Live in Subjection One to Another (Epistle 99, 1655)

Introductory Note

This excerpt begins with the condemnation of all "foolish" and "frothy" thoughts—the first step to the subjection of our minds to Christ. Then, Fox says, we "come into the authority of God." Fox provocatively contrasts this with "usurped authority," which today we see in race, class, or gender privilege. Fox refutes the false doctrine that the man is the head of the woman by declaring that Christ is equally "head" in men and women. Fox's alternative to usurped authority is to live under the authority of God. Practically speaking, this means living in "subjection one to another."

It is worth sitting for a while with the extraordinary metaphor, "then ye come to be bone of his bone and flesh of his flesh." What does it mean to be bone of Christ's bone, flesh of Christ's flesh?

This epistle was originally titled, *To all that make mention of the name of the Lord, and that profess his living truth*.

Scripture

Yea, all *of you* be subject one to another, and be clothed
with humility: for God resisteth the proud, and giveth grace
to the humble. Humble yourselves therefore under the
mighty hand of God, that he may exalt you in due time.
1 Peter 5:5–6 (KJV)

And the LORD God said, *It is* not good that the man should be alone;
I will make him an help meet for him. . . . And Adam said, This is now
bone of my bones, and flesh of my flesh: she shall be called Woman.
Genesis 2:18, 23 (KJV)

Epistle

Friends,—

A warning and charge to you all
from the presence of the living God, to

let all lightness and airiness,
foolishness, wilfulness, and frothiness
be judged in patience;

let it come to the fire and be burned,
and hay, wood, and stubble,
and all that which is above the seed;

he that builds there, is above the foundation,
his works are to be burned,
he will suffer loss.

So all come into the authority of God,
which is not usurped,
which gives the dominion over all the usurped authority;

that ye may live all in the one power of the son of God,
which brings all into the unity
and subdues all things that cause the enmity. . . .

So all power is given to the son
to rule, to subdue, and to judge.

So, live in the power,
and ye live in the unity,
ye live in the peace,

ye live all in the subjection
one to another
in the fear of the Lord;

ye live all in the seed, which is one,
which keeps atop of the head of the serpent,
and keeps his head down, and bringeth it under.

So, feel the seed of God in every particular
to be the head in the male and in the female,
and then ye come to be
        bone of his bone,
        and flesh of his flesh,

and to inherit every one
the promise of God in the particular. . . .

If Any Be Oppressed (Epistle 121, 1656)

Introductory Note

Originally titled, *To take care of such who suffer for owning the truth*, this epistle combines the beauty of a psalm with the practicality of a bulleted memo. It was Fox's genius to blend the practical business of care of the poor and oppressed in contemporary England with the biblical story of creation where everything was good. This is what it means to be governed by "the wisdom of God." We do not live in a time when Friends, as such, are oppressed, though many Friends continue to experience hardship for Truth's sake. The Gospel is always counter-cultural and in times of "wind" and "storm," we could heed Fox's admonition to help one another, as "family."

Scripture

And he shall judge the world in righteousness,
he shall minister judgment to the people in uprightness.
The LORD also will be a refuge for the oppressed,
a refuge in times of trouble.
Psalm 9:8–9 (KJV)

Epistle

Friends,—

Dwell in the wisdom and power of God,
by which all things must be ordered to his glory,
in which ye may do all things to his glory;

and that with the wisdom of God
ye may order and preserve the creation,
and every thing that is good.

And if any servants be convinced, and turned from their places for truth's sake, Friends to be tender to them, that they be not lost; but that they may be preserved.

And if any soldiers be put out of the army for truth's sake, that they may be nourished and cherished;

or any children be turned from their parents,

or believing wives from their unbelieving husbands, that they may be admonished to walk wisely towards them.

And that all prisoners, that have but little of their own, there may be care taken for them,

and for the lame and sick.

And that if any Friends
be oppressed any manner of way,
others may take care to help them.

And that all may be as one family,
building up one another,
and helping one another. . . .

And all Friends every where,
in the power, and life, and seed of God
keep your meetings,

that over all the top-stone may be laid,
and ye all in the wisdom and patience
may be preserved,

and as a sweet savour may be kept to God,
and in the hearts of all people.

And every one be obedient
to the life and power of the Lord God,
and that will keep you from being as a wilderness;

but be faithful and still,
till the winds cease,
and the storm be over.

Silence All Flesh: Beware of Contention (Epistle 122, 1656)

Introductory Note

Fox addresses disagreement and debate within the faith community and warns Friends not to "strive about words." This epistle was written about the time of the controversy surrounding James Nayler (see Ni:268–269; Healey:297ff). Fox draws the crucial distinction between those who argue "to exercise lordship" and those who are "low and wait upon God." Unity is to be found only through "that of God in the conscience," not through will or the power of one's logic or reason—which is "the seat for mastery and pride."

Note: Fox twice speaks of the fear of the Lord. This does not refer to anxiety about an angry or vengeful God but rather refers to an inner sense of awe of the One who created all things good and whose love is everlasting.

Also, note: At the end, Fox does not appeal to conscience itself, which is shaped by culture, but to "that of God in the conscience," which is where Christ, the inward Teacher, resides.

Scripture

And there shall in no wise enter into it any thing that defileth.
Revelation 21:27 (KJV)

You must understand this, my beloved: let everyone be quick to listen, slow to speak, slow to anger; for your anger does not produce God's righteousness.
James 1:19–20 (NRS)

Epistle

Friends,—

To that which is pure, I speak,
in which is unity,
where no defiled thing shall enter.

Silence all flesh,
who strive about words,
in which is no profit;

who would draw you out of your conditions,
and others out of their conditions.

Therefore be low,
and mind that which is low,
to draw you out of contention.

And strive not for mastery,
and do not exercise lordship over one another;
but mind that which is pure,
which keeps you in the fear of the Lord God.

For if your minds go from that which is pure,
  which leads to God,
  your nakedness will appear to the world;

and then ye go in your own wills and strength,
and there is the seat for mastery and pride,
  out of the will of God,
  and that is out of the unity,

out of the oneness,
out of the way;

and instead of building, ye destroy;
and instead of edifying, ye draw back into the world.

Therefore all be low, and wait upon the Lord,
and be swift to hear,
slow to speak,
and slow to wrath;

be low, and wait upon God,
to receive the living food from God,
to nourish you in time,
with that which was before time;
that God in all things may be glorified.

So meet together and wait upon God,
if there be not a word,

I charge you.

Beware of contention,
for there ye get above that of God
in the conscience,

and so go out of the fear of the Lord.

In Christ the Seed, Is Peace (Epistle 123, 1656)

Introductory Note

Originally titled, *Men in the fall are in the wars and strife, but truth restores and brings into peace*. This epistle gives us the root of the Quaker peace testimony. Wars and fighting are the expression of the worldly passions (lusts) that separated humankind from God. Peace and healing are (only) to be found in those who have "come to the witness of God in themselves." Fox reaches forward to the Tree of Life (whose leaves are for "the healing of the nations," Revelation 22:2) and turns to Christ, "the second Adam," where is "the rest, and the peace, and the life" (Genesis 2:9).

T. Canby Jones (Jones:xviii) points out that 1 Corinthians 15:45 is the likely scriptural basis for Fox referring to Christ as the second Adam. It is as the second Adam that Christ returns us to the condition of the first Adam before his disobedience.

Scripture

In the midst of the street of it, and on either side of the river, *was there* the tree of life, which bare twelve *manner of* fruits, *and* yielded her fruit every month: and the leaves of the tree *were* for the healing of the nations.
Revelation 22:2 (KJV)

And so it is written, The first man Adam was made a living soul; the last Adam *was made* a quickening spirit.
1 Corinthians 15:45 (KJV)

Epistle

Dear Friends,—

My love is to you all
in the everlasting seed of God,
that never changes nor falls, . . .

and the seed is not as the corn
that grows upon the house top, that withers;
for the leaves that this seed brings forth,
never fade nor fall;
for the leaves thereof
heal the nations which are wounded.

The second Adam goes over Adam in the fall, and his quarreling sons and daughters, who war one with another with their carnal weapons. . . . But [those] who are in the noble and royal seed, are all in peace, and in love, and in life, and in unity. . . .

In this seed, Christ,
is peace and rest,
    out of all troubles,
    out of all whimsies, foolish dreams,
    imaginations, fancies
    false visions, false revelations.

For the seed, in which the blessing is,
is felt,
    and the life,
    and the light,
    and the righteousness,
    and the truth,
that answers the witness of God
    in all men and women,
    (whether they will hear or forbear).

And so, all that are in Adam in the fall,
    both men and women,
    and there remaining in the fall,
they never are in rest nor peace,
    but are in travails, wars, strife, fightings;
    the lusts being the ground of all this. . . .

For in Adam in the fall
    is all the inward foul weather,
    storms, tempests, winds, strifes,

the whole family of it in confusion,
    being all gone from the spirit
    and the witness of God in themselves,
    and the power and the light;

in which power, light, and spirit
    is the fellowship with God
    and one with another,

through which they come out of Adam in the fall,
into the second Adam that never fell. . . .

So they have no peace nor rest
in the old Adam in the fall,

but in the second Adam,
Christ, that never fell,
    are the rest,
    and the peace,
    and the life. . . .

"My Business, My Business" (Epistle 131, 1656)

Introductory Note

This epistle is notable for Fox's recollection of the hardships endured by early Quaker businesses when they insisted on a fair price for their products rather than bargaining and how this later brought success. Fox addresses the temptation to put the blessings of God ahead of God and thus to become entangled in the affairs of life ("striving about earthly things"). Fox appended the instruction: Let this be read in your meetings.

Note: When Fox counsels Friends against "jars and strife," he is using "jars" in an earlier sense of "dissension, quarreling" (OED). When Fox cautions against "going up and down to minister" unless led by God, he is referring to Friends traveling here and there to preach the gospel in marketplaces, churches, and so forth.

Scripture

But He said to him, "A certain man was giving a big dinner, and
he invited many; . . . But they all alike began to make excuses.
The first one said to him, 'I have bought a piece of land and
I need to go out and look at it; please consider me excused.'
And another one said, 'I have bought five yoke of oxen, and I
am going to try them out; please consider me excused.'"
Luke 14:16, 18–19 (NAS)

Epistle

Friends every where,

dwell in the power of the Lord God,
which is without end,
in which ye may all have unity.

And take heed of striving about earthly things,
which is the unredeemed part,
that is out of the paradise and the garden of God;

but that with the wisdom of God
ye may come to be ordered,
and order the creatures by that
by which they were made and created,
that by it ye may know yourselves to be governed.

And after that riches increase,
take heed of setting your hearts upon them,
lest they become a curse and a plague to you.

For when ye were faithful at the first, the world would refrain from you, and not have commerce with you; but after, when they saw ye were faithful and just in things, and righteous and honest in your tradings and dealings, then they came to have commerce and trade with you the more, because they know ye will not cozen them, nor cheat them: then ye came to have greater trading, double than ever ye had, and more than the world.

But there is the danger and temptation to you, of drawing your minds into your business, and clogging them with it; so that ye can hardly do any thing to the service of God, but there will be crying, my business, my business; and your minds will go into the things, and not over the things; and so therein ye do not come into the image of God, in which is dominion. And so, when your minds are got into the riches, and cumbered therewith, ye go back into that ye were in before—and then, if the Lord God cross you, and stop you by sea and land, and take your goods and customers from you, that your minds should not be cumbered; then that mind that is cumbered, will fret, being out of the power of God.

And all Friends, take heed of jars and strife, for that is it which will eat out the seed in you; therefore . . . dwell in love and life, and in the power and seed of God. . . .

And all Friends every where, if Friends be poor, and in want, or in prison, that ye may in wisdom relieve and cherish such. . . .

And all Friends every where, take heed of wronging the world, or any one, in bargains, or overreaching them; but dwell in the cool, sweet, and holy power of the Lord God, and in righteousness, that it may run down amongst you; and that will keep you low.

And all Friends every where, take heed of slothfulness and sleeping in your meetings; for in so doing ye will be bad examples to others, and hurt yourselves and them.

And all take heed of going up and down to minister, but as ye are moved of the Lord God, or to speak in meetings, or any other places. . . .

> And dwell in the seed,
> that ye all may know Christ
> come to reign in you;
>
> so that all may be done and spoken
> by and in the power of the Lord God, . . .
> and not out of it: . . .

that ye may come to know the place where there is no curse,
and the Lamb's power, throne, life, and dominion.

And in the wisdom of God all dwell,
that to him ye may be a sweet savour,
and a blessing in the hearts of all people;

that nothing may rule nor reign amongst you,
but the seed itself,
and the life of God.

Mind the Chaste Life! (Epistle 154, 1657)

Introductory Note

"Chastity" refers both to a life that is sexually pure and, more generally, to a life that is morally virtuous. Fox calls for holiness and chastity as a testimony that Christ's power enables us to live lives ordered by the wisdom of God, "for in that is the unity, and out of that is the war."

Note: For Fox, the "bride of Christ" is a metaphor for the faithful of any gender. Also note that Fox concludes this appeal for Friends to live "pure" and "chaste" with a warning against being judgmental, which he says should be "judged down."

Scripture

From whence *come* wars and fightings among you? *come they* not hence, *even* of your lusts that war in your members?
James 4:1 (KJV)

Let us be glad and rejoice, and give honour to him: for the marriage of the Lamb is come, and his wife hath made herself ready. And to her was granted that she should be arrayed in fine linen, clean and white: for the fine linen is the righteousness of saints.
Revelation 19:7–8 (KJV)

Epistle

O friends!

keep out of that state,
which is out of and below
the chaste nature;

for all unchasteness,
by the power of the Lord
and his truth and light,
is to be judged.

Therefore live in the truth
and in the light of God,
that keeps you all chaste,

for in that is the unity,
and out of that is the war.
For from the lusts are the wars and strife.

Oh!

keep over that nature,
        that purity may flow,
        and righteousness spread,
        and truth flourish,
        and love and peace abound
in and amongst all the family of God.

Keep down the unchaste,
keep down the adulterous eye,
and keep down the lust of the flesh,
which is not of the Father but of the world. . . .

Oh! therefore

mind the holy life, the chaste life!

That is the bride's clothing,
by which she adorns herself
for her husband, Christ Jesus.

Therefore

live in that which keeps your peace,
there is your life and dominion;
that weeds may not grow, nor brambles,
but that they all may be cut down and weeded out.

For those grow through the liberty of the flesh,
and by that ye come to be darkened,
and lose your discerning and feeling;
and there gets the beam into the eye,

by which ye come to judge
with that judgment which is for judgment,
which should be judged down
by the spirit of truth and peace. . . .

Do Not Be Choked with Cares (Epistle 161, 1658)

Introductory Note

Fox is not a Franciscan, urging Friends to embrace lady poverty as a spiritual discipline. However, he does caution against being "married" to material things and urges, instead, "to be free and loose from them" and be "married" to Christ. These are images worth sitting with.

Scripture

And that which fell among thorns are they, which, when they have heard, go forth, and are choked with cares and riches and pleasures of *this* life, and bring no fruit to perfection. But that on the good ground are they, which in an honest and good heart, having heard the word, keep *it*, and bring forth fruit with patience.

Luke 8:14–15 (KJV)

Epistle

O friends! do not die from the good
through the wantonness of fleshly lusts,
neither be choked with the cares of this life,
nor fear the shearers,

neither let the heat scorch your green blade;
but dwell under the shadow of the Almighty,
who will shade you from the heat and cold.

Neither be cumbered nor surfeited
with the riches of this world,
nor bound, nor straitened with them,
nor married to them;

but be free and loose from them,
and be married to the Lord.

Live in Unity, Peace, and Love (Epistle 163, 1658)

Introductory Note

In 1658, Fox writes to Friends in the face of political and social turmoil. The future of the Commonwealth was cast in doubt when Oliver Cromwell died and his politically weaker son, Richard, was named Protector. Many Friends were suffering in prison.

In such times, Fox urges Friends to live in a loving and united community—in the light, life, and power of God. Fox uses a double metaphor for Christ whom he calls "the Seed" and "the top-stone" (a synonym for "cap-stone"). The Seed, is "set over all" (has power over) all the causes of suffering. The Top-stone, "laid over all," completes the structure and holds everything together. In these times of turmoil and suffering, Fox's advice is "feel" the Seed and Top-stone and "live" in the power of God over all.

Note: the repeated phrase, "which was before," brings Friends to Eden before "the fall."

Scripture

> I therefore, the prisoner of the Lord, beseech you that ye walk worthy of the vocation wherewith ye are called, With all lowliness and meekness, with longsuffering, forbearing one another in love; Endeavouring to keep the unity of the Spirit in the bond of peace.
>
> Ephesians 4:1–3 (KJV)

Epistle

My dear friends,—

Live
in the life
in which is the unity and peace
one with another,

and lowliness and humbleness
of heart and mind. . . .

And so,
this is the word of the Lord God
to you all:

live
in the power of the Lord God,
in which is peace, love, unity,
and dominion

in the life
and power of God,
which was before enmity was;

and in the light,
which was before darkness was;

and in the life,
which was before death was:

and so, in that
feel unity and life
in the power of God.

And so, the seed of God
feel over all that set,
which makes to suffer;

which was before it was,
and will remain
when that is all gone.

And so,
feel the top-stone over all laid,
that his life ye may feel over all,

and in that live.

To All Friends, Prisoners (Epistle 204, 1661)

Introductory Note

Fox wrote *To all Friends, prisoners from London, the 22 nd of the 3 d month, 1661*. Several thousand Friends were, at this time, cast in prison, suspected of joining the Fifth Monarchy Men's uprising against the newly reinstated King Charles II. Friends tried to clear their name by issuing their well-known peace testimony ("All bloody principles and practices, we . . . utterly deny" [Ni:399]). In the midst of political and social turmoil, Fox's counsel to suffering Friends was to return to the seed (Christ) and wait to feel the power of God, which brings "to the beginning, where is life."

Note: Fox uses the word "power" ten times in this selection. It is worth tracing what he says about power as he writes to imprisoned and powerless Friends.

Scripture

Who hath saved us, and called *us* with an holy calling, not according to our works, but according to his own purpose and grace, which was given us in Christ Jesus before the world began, But is now made manifest by the appearing of our Saviour Jesus Christ, who hath abolished death, and hath brought life and immortality to light through the gospel.
2 Timothy 1:9–10 (KJV)

And to make all *men* see what *is* the fellowship of the mystery, which from the beginning of the world hath been hid in God, who created all things by Jesus Christ: To the intent that now unto the principalities and powers in heavenly *places* might be known by the church the manifold wisdom of God.
Ephesians 3:9–10 (KJV)

Epistle

Dear friends and brethren,—

The seed of God feel all in yourselves,
which is the heir of the power of God, . . .
In which power of God is the fellowship, . . .
which brings life and immortality to light. . . .

So walk in the truth,
then ye walk with the God of all truth;

and walk in the righteousness,
and then ye walk with the righteous God in all peace . . .

Therefore walk in the power of God,
which goes over the power of darkness,
which was before it was;
which power of God is the gospel,
in which is the mystery of the fellowship
a mystery (I say) to all the fellowships
that are out of the power of God. . . .

So in that meet, in the seed,
in that wait, in the power of God,
in which ye have life,

in that keep your meetings;
which brings to feel that, which was
before the power of darkness was.

And wait to inherit the wisdom of God,

that with that ye may all be ordered
to God's glory in his life,

in which ye may feel unity
with himself, and one with another,

and his presence and blessings among you,
in the power and seed of God. . . .

Which power of God
brings from all the barren mountains,
where is death,

to the beginning,
where is life.

Gathered in the Name of Jesus (Epistle 209, 1661)

Introductory Note

In this epistle, written *From Mendlesham, this 11 th day of the 1 st month*. and addressed *To Friends, in and about Norfolk and Lyn, &c.*, Fox exalts the name of Jesus, "whose name is above every name." This is the other side of the doctrine of the universal saving Light expressed, for instance, in Epistle 388. (See Robert Barclay's *Barclay's Apology in Modern English*, edited by Dean Freidy, 1967, pages 172–175, for a theological synthesis of this paradox.) What feelings rise up for you as you contemplate gathering in the name of Jesus?

Scripture

> He humbled himself, and became obedient unto death, even the death of the cross. Wherefore God also hath highly exalted him, and given him a name which is above every name.
>
> Philippians 2:8–9 (KJV)

Epistle

My dear friends,—In the power of God and his immortal seed dwell, in which ye all will have life eternal . . .

> In this live and dwell,
> in which ye will all have unity and fellowship;
> in which ye will feel life eternal amongst you.
>
> In that meet and keep your meetings,
> and wait together upon the Lord,
> who are gathered together in the name of Jesus;
> whose name is above every name.
>
> So is his gathering above all other gatherings;
> which gathering stands
> when all other gatherings are ended.

And not in any other name
under heaven is salvation brought,
but in the name of Jesus;

in which name are your gatherings;
in which name ye all know your salvation,
        and shall all know it;
as ye abide all in the power of God,
that keeps unto the day of salvation. . . .

And the Lord God Almighty preserve you, and keep you. So my love in the everlasting seed of God is to you all.

Friends in Ireland: Send News! (Epistle 218, 1662)

Introductory Note:

This epistle, addressed *To Friends in Ireland*, carries an urgent plea for news. It is a curious fact that, when one divides the text of the letter into two, equal, side-by-side columns, remarkable parallels are revealed. Each half begins with a greeting and corresponding words of faith. The central sections begin or end with "keep your meetings" and "dwell in the power . . . of God," and both concern hardship or persecution. In the first half, fear of "amazements" in the sea become, in the second half, God's "rod" against the "persecutors." Both halves conclude with words about "unity." Writing from Swarthmoor Hall, Fox appears to be on tenterhooks to hear how Friends in Ireland are faring. The concluding lines of each half can be joined to become a command to send news, "this is the word of the Lord"!

Scripture

And ye shall be hated of all *men* for my name's sake. But there shall not an hair of your head perish. In your patience possess ye your souls.
Luke 21:17–19 (KJV)

Epistle

Dear friends and brethren,—
Let patience possess your souls,
and in the seed of God dwell;
that over all the top-stone may be laid and set.
And the kingdom of peace dwell in, which hath no end;
in which ye will feel the Supreme Head:
and in the power of the Lord

keep your meetings, which was before the waves were, or winds either. So in that look over all, and keep in the faith, by which ye will have access to God over that which separates from God; in that ye will have unity, and will not fear the amazements which are in the sea, because of the winds, and storms, and blusterings,

who know the election
which was before the world began.

And live in peace
and unity in that,
and send over how things are among you. (I am in the north, at Swarthmore.)

And, dear friends and brethren,
be not troubled,
but dwell in the seed of God,
which goeth over all this;
and remains and stands when all this blustering is ended and gone.

Therefore look at the Lord above all,
and his arm:

for God had a rod in secret, to fetch down these persecutors, who have long reigned in their wickedness, until they were neither fit for God, nor man hardly. So again, God hath a rod in reserve, to bring down these spirits, which have been a rod. Therefore all dwell in the power and spirit of God, with which ye will comprehend all that which is to change,

with that
which doth not change, and hath no end;
in that live, and ye will have
an everlasting unity:
and to you this is the word of the Lord God.

Abide in Christ, by Whom the World Was Made (Epistle 221, 1662)

Introductory Note

This letter was sent *The 10 th day of the 11 th month, 1662*, during the period of persecution under The Quaker Act that outlawed attendance at Friends meetings where five or more assembled. Thousands were imprisoned, and several died from the vile conditions. Fox urges Friends to keep their first "habitation," which is safe and powerful in the face of all these dangers.

Scripture

The name of the LORD is a strong tower: the
righteous runneth into it, and is safe.
Proverbs 18:10 (KJV)

But they shall sit every man under his vine and under
his fig tree; and none shall make *them* afraid: for the
mouth of the LORD of hosts hath spoken *it*.
Micah 4:4 (KJV)

Epistle

My dear friends, . . .

keep your first habitations
in the power of the Lord God,
and in his light, and life, and spirit,

by which all your minds may be stayed,
and kept up to the Lord God,
in the unchangeable
light, life, power, and spirit.

And so ye living
in the unchangeable life and light,
ye see Christ, that does not change,
but ends all changeable things,
types, figures, and shadows,

and destroys the author of
all evil inventions and traditions
among all the sons and daughters of Adam
in the fall;

and so live all up in the royal seed,
in which ye have life,
which life was before death;
walking in the light,
which was before darkness,
and in the power of God,
which was before the power of darkness was. . . .

Therefore mind the power of God . . . and feel Christ to reign amongst you, who is the prince of peace and life; and this will keep you from being tossed and carried about with strange doctrines, . . . in a pretence of new discoveries. . . .

Therefore mind the spirit of truth, and the unfeigned love . . . and the fellowship of the gospel, which is the power of God;

which power of God was
before the power of satan was,
in that live, and meet and walk
in the name of the Lord,

which is a strong tower,
(whose name is the power,)
and in the tower is the safety
over wickedness, and before it was;

sitting under your own vine, and abiding in it,
then ye abide in Christ,

by whom the world was made,
who is the light, life, and truth,
        and the power of God;

and as ye abide there,
ye bear fruit to the glory of God,
and through him ye come every one
to have a habitation in God,

who brings out of the fall,
        where the curse is,
to the state that man was in before he fell,
        and to the blessing,
and not only to that state,
        but to him that never fell,

in whom the saints sit down,
in whom are the pastures of life,
and riches eternal, everlasting,
and the blessing of the Lord,
        that with that ye may be clothed.

And so farewell! My love to all Friends. . . .

Worship in Spirit and Truth (Epistle 222, 1662)

Introductory Note

This epistle provides a remarkable summary of Quaker insight into true Christian worship. It served as a defense of Quaker gatherings for worship in the face of The Quaker Act, which made such gatherings illegal. The sixth section, on Singing in the Spirit, leads into a powerful poem on "hearing the voice of Christ." It is a good reminder of the core experience of Christian worship.

This excerpt is from a much longer epistle originally titled, *A general epistle to be read in all the christian meetings in the world. Blessed is he that readeth, and blessed is he that heareth and understandeth, and the eyes that see. Read this over, and you may read that which you have not read, and see that which you have not seen*. Fox notes that he was writing *From Cockford in Essex the 12 th day of the 11 th month, 1662*. The paragraph numbering (originally beginning "2dly," with the second paragraph) is given in the 1831 edition of Fox, *Works*. I have added the subject headings.

Scripture

> But the hour cometh, and now is, when the true worshippers shall worship the Father in spirit and in truth: for the Father seeketh such to worship him. God *is* a Spirit: and they that worship him must worship *him* in spirit and in truth.
> John 4:23–24 (KJV)

> I am the good shepherd: the good shepherd giveth his life for the sheep. But he that is an hireling, and not the shepherd, whose own the sheep are not, seeth the wolf coming, and leaveth the sheep, and fleeth: and the wolf catcheth them, and scattereth the sheep. The hireling fleeth, because he is an hireling, and careth not for the sheep. I am the good shepherd, and know my *sheep*, and am known of mine. As the Father knoweth me, even so know I the Father: and I lay down my life for the sheep.
> John 10:11–15 (KJV)

Epistle

My dear friends all every where, in the seed dwell. . . .

[1stly. The name of Jesus]

And so you that are gathered in the name of Jesus . . . for his name sake have ye suffered all along by many powers; his name is a strong tower, . . . and gathered in the name of the Lord, ye are in the strong tower, in which is safety and peace; . . . and not by any other name under heaven, but by the name of Jesus Christ is salvation brought, by whom all things were made. . . . Now . . . all things in heaven, and things in earth, must bow at the name of Jesus, before they be reconciled to God. . . . So bow at the name of Jesus.

2dly. [The cross of Christ]

You must bow at the cross of Christ, which is the power of God, which since the apostles' days the apostate christians have lost; and therefore they bow to a cross, a stick, a stone, a piece of iron, a piece of wood. . . . So bow to the power of God . . . that crosseth down the earthly, carnal, ungodly part in man and woman, and works over it, and strikes over it, and goes over it, and crosseth it. There is the mystery. . . .

3dly. [The fellowship of the Gospel]

The fellowship of the gospel, the power of God, expels away all that which hath darkened the understanding, darkened the mind, darkened the heart . . . And here is the joyful gospel, and here is the faith in the everlasting gospel, the power of God; and here is life and immortality come to light through the power of God, (the gospel,) . . . [and] here you are church members, and here you are living stones, and here you are built up together a spiritual household; here the church in God is known, . . . The church in God will stand, the pillar and ground of truth, and the fellowship of it will remain. Therefore, ye heirs of the gospel, . . . set down in the fellowship of the same. . . .

4thly. [Worship in Spirit and truth]

The worship of God is in the spirit and in the truth, that is the public worship which Christ set up; . . . and said, "God is a spirit; and they that worship him, must worship him in spirit and truth; and the hour is come, and now is, that the Father seeks such to worship him." Then the hour was, that worship was set up, above sixteen hundred years since . . . This is the public worship, and . . . worship in the spirit and in the truth, . . . brings every man and woman to the spirit of God in their own hearts, and truth in their inward parts; in which spirit and truth they must bow down. . . .

5thly. [Prayer in the Spirit]

To pray in the spirit, . . . is the public prayer set up by the apostles: every man, every woman then must come to the spirit of God in their own selves; for it will give them understanding and knowledge, and give them instruction, it will help their infirmities, it will let them see their wants: . . . for Christ the quickening spirit, and the spirit of the Lord within, is that which brings people to lift up their eyes to the Lord in spirit and truth, and to watch and pray, by which they know temptations; and the spirit giveth them understanding, and wisdom, and power to withstand them.

6thly. [Singing in the Spirit]

Singing in the spirit is public; every man and every woman in the whole world, they must not grieve it, nor vex it, if they sing in it; and this is public. But they that go from the spirit of God within, they go into the particular singing, inventing this thing and that thing, and then one will do it, and another will not do it, and so there is no true fellowship, because it is not done in the spirit; . . . for the true fellowship in singing, in praying, in worshipping of God, is in the spirit of God, . . . for in that is the bond of peace. . . .

So all Friends, be faithful and valiant for the truth of God upon the earth. For there are religions only for the summer, . . . but when the storm comes, their flight is in the winter. . . . Therefore mind ye the power of God, that ye may bear fruit in winter, and sit under your vine, Christ Jesus, that ye may see before winter storms and tempests were, and to that which shall never have an end, nor change;

in this is the pure religion. . . .

hearing the voice of Christ,
which is the light,
the light's voice,
the life's voice,
the truth's voice,

the power of God's voice,
which goes before you,

through which ye may have
life eternal. . . .

[C]hristendom have more minded the hireling's voice,
than Christ the light's voice,
the truth's voice,
the voice of the life and power of God
in themselves;

they have gone from that,
and gone to the voice of the hireling,
who flies when the wolf comes,
and leaves his flock, and cares not for it.

Therefore you that have heard the voice of Christ,
who are his sheep, and follow him; . . .
follow him still,
and he will give you life eternal,
for he is the rest. . . .

All keep to the beauty of holiness;
for in holiness lies your beauty;
and the fruits of righteousness
is a tree of life,

and the name of the Lord is a strong tower,
and the righteous flee into it,
and are safe.

Choose the Better Thing (Epistle 230, 1663)

Introductory Note

Often, when Fox reads scripture, he sees it pointing to an inward experience. Here, he is sitting, like Mary, at Jesus' feet, hearing Jesus teaching about "the one good." This epistle could almost serve as Fox's credo for the true faith.

Scripture

Now it came to pass, as they went, that he entered into a certain village: and a certain woman named Martha received him into her house. And she had a sister called Mary, which also sat at Jesus' feet, and heard his word. . . . But one thing is needful: and Mary hath chosen that good part, which shall not be taken away from her.
Luke 10:38–39, 42 (KJV)

While ye have light, believe in the light, that
ye may be the children of light.
John 12:36 (KJV)

Epistle

Friends,—

Stand still and see,
be still and hear,
sit at Jesus' feet,
and choose the better thing; . . .

there is no true religion
but what is pure from above; . . .

and there is no true church
but where Christ exercises his offices . . .;

none come to be children of the light
but such as believe in the light;

no sons of God,
but by receiving Christ, and by being led by his spirit;

no purifying,
but by coming to Christ, the hope of glory, the purifier;

and no overcoming,
but by believing in Christ the light,
and he that doth so is born of God.

And there is no true witness within
but the light, the life, and spirit of Christ, the true record;

no true faith
but that which Christ is the author of, which giveth victory; . . .

no salvation,
but by the name of Jesus;

no true praying,
but in the spirit;

no true singing,
but in the spirit;

no true fast,
but that which breaks the bond of iniquity;

no true fellowship,
but in the pure faith, light, spirit, and gospel of God and Christ;

no true foundation,
but Christ, to build upon;

no true way,
but Christ;

no true seed,
but what Christ hath sown in the heart; . . .

no true peace,
but in Christ; . . .

no knowing the things of God,
but by the spirit of God;

no knowing the son nor the Father,
but by the revelation of the holy spirit;

no knowing the scriptures,
but by the same holy ghost that moved the holy men to give
them forth;

no calling Jesus, Lord,
but by the holy ghost, by which he was conceived; . . .

no true wisdom,
but from above;

and no true receiving it,
but in the fear of the Lord; . . .

and no true love to God,
but what he sheddeth abroad in the heart;

and to know a fellowship with Christ
in his death and sufferings,
is above the fellowship of bread and wine,
which will have an end;
but the fellowship in the gospel and holy spirit
hath no end.

Follow Christ's Way of Peace (Epistle 234, 1664)

Introductory Note

Does being "meek and low" work when you are dealing with people who appear to only understand the language of force and violence? The question—frequently heard in arguments about the effectiveness of nonviolence considered as a political tactic—misses the fact that "the followers of the Lamb" are already "in the prince of peace's kingdom" and share in the victory he has already won. Violence on the part of followers of the Lamb would subvert the dominion of the Prince of Peace. It is worth noting that being "meek and low" does not mean false humility or accommodation with evil. Fox is, after all, addressing people in prison for having boldly and publicly stood up for their faith.

Scripture

I gave my back to the smiters, and my cheeks to them that plucked off the hair: I hid not my face from shame and spitting. For the Lord GOD will help me; therefore shall I not be confounded.
Isaiah 50:6–7 (KJV)

And they overcame him by the blood of the Lamb, and by the word of their testimony; and they loved not their lives unto the death.
Revelation 12:11 (KJV)

Epistle

[The Lamb's Victory]

All you prisoners of the Lord
for his truth's sake,
and for keeping the testimony of Jesus Christ. . . .

Your patience must overcome
all these rough and hasty spirits in the world,
and your love must bear all things;

for patience obtains the crown
which is immortal,
which runs the race.

So it is the Lamb must have the victory
over all the unclean airy spirits,
and over him that is out of the truth.

[The Example of Christ]

So, be meek and low,
then you follow the example of Christ,
and come to bear the image of the just,
who suffered by the unjust;

and put on his righteousness,
who suffered by the unrighteous;
    whose back was struck,
    and his hair was plucked off,
    and face was spit upon,

and yet cried, "Father forgive them."
Here he kept his dominion,
    a sufferer who had the victory,
    which the followers of the lamb
    do in measure attain unto.

[The Power of God]

So put on courage,
put on patience.

Let your loyalty be known;
for your king that hath conquered
the devil, death, and hell,

in walking in righteousness, peace, and truth,
feeling the power of God,
teaching every one of you
when words are not uttered.

And let your faith be in the power
that goes through all things,
and over all things,
and every one hearken to it. . . .

And this is the power of God,
in which you feel to before enmity was,
and be at peace one with another,

then you live
in the prince of peace's
kingdom, and dominion,
          and life;

in which is unity,
which was before enmity was,
which destroys it. . . .

All men and women's strength
is in the power of God;
that goes over the power of darkness.

So feel all this to go through all, and over all, preaching and working in you; . . . And by it feel the seed raised up in one another. . . .

To All Women's Meetings (Epistle 291, 1672)

Introductory Note

The equality of women and men was among the first testimonies of Friends and was demonstrated in the prominent and controversial leadership roles of women such as Elizabeth Hooton, Margaret Fell, Mary Fisher, Mary Dyer, and many others whose prophetic preaching some found scandalous but had a major part in spreading the everlasting gospel. In this epistle, addressed *To all the women's meetings, that are believers in the truth*, Fox asserts the equality of women and men in leadership and encourages "your women's meetings." (See also, Epistle 320.) The foundational theological idea is that Christ restores men and women to the state of Adam and Eve, who were equal "help-meets" before the fall.

Note: Five years prior to this, in 1667, Margaret Fell, then a prisoner in Lancaster Castle prison, wrote the seminal tract, "Women's Speaking Justified." Fox and Fell married each other in 1669.

Scripture

And the LORD God said, *It is* not good that the man should be alone; I will make him an help meet for him.
Genesis 2:18 (KJV)

So God created man in his *own* image, in the image of God created he him; male and female created he them.
Genesis 1:27 (KJV)

Epistle

Friends,—

Keep your women's meetings in the power of God . . . and keep the gospel order.

For man and woman were helps-meet in the image of God, and in righteousness and holiness, in the dominion, before they fell; but after the fall in the transgression, the man was to rule over his wife; but in the restoration by Christ, into the image of God, and his righteousness and holiness again, in that they are helps-meet, man and woman, as they were before the fall. . . .

And women are to take up the cross daily,
and follow Christ daily,
as well as the men;

and so to be taught of him their prophet,
and fed of him their shepherd,
and counselled of him their counsellor,
and sanctified by him
who offered up himself once for all. . . .

Mary Magdalene, and the other Mary, were the first preachers of Christ's resurrection to the disciples, and the disciples could not believe their message and testimony that they had from Jesus, as some now-a-days cannot; but they received the command, and being sent preached it.

So is every woman and man to do, that sees him risen, and has the command and message; daughters shall prophesy as well as sons.

So they are to be obedient, that have the spirit poured upon them. Women are to prophesy; and prophecy is not to be quenched. They that have the testimony of Jesus, are commanded to keep it, whether men or women. . . .

So women are to keep in the government of Christ, and to be obeyers of Christ; and women are to keep the comely order of the gospel, as well as men, and to see that all that have received Christ Jesus, that they walk in Christ Jesus . . . of the increase of whose government there is no end.

So the foundation of our women's meetings is Christ, to all them that be heirs of him, and of his government . . . and therefore, I say, take your possessions of it, and walk as becomes the gospel; and keep the comely order of it, and in it keep your meetings. . . .

So . . . both men and women, be helps-meet in the image of God, in the righteousness and holiness in the restoration. . . . And so see that nothing be lacking amongst you, then all will be well.

Postscript.—

And the elder women in the truth
were not only called elders, but mothers.

Now a mother in the church of Christ,
and a mother in Israel,
  is one that gives suck,
  and nourishes, and feeds,
  and washes, and rules,

and is a teacher, in the church,
and in the Israel of God,

and an admonisher,
an instructer, an exhorter.

So, all that are come to that office,
growth, and stature,

be diligent;

for a mother in Israel, or in the church of Christ,
is beyond all the mothers in Egypt, and in Sodom,
and the mother of harlots, mystery Babylon,
who had power over tongues, nations, and people,
with the cup of her fornication.

But the mothers in spiritual Israel, and church of Christ,
has the cup of salvation,
and the breasts of consolation,
which are full of the milk of the word,
to suckle all the young ones,
and to nourish, and instruct,
admonish, and exhort,
and rebuke all the contrary;

and to refresh and cherish
every tender one. . . .

The Living God (Epistle 292, 1672)

Introductory Note

Fox addressed this epistle *To Friends in New England, Virginia, and Barbados*, where he was traveling during the period 1671–1673. In his *Journal*, Fox recounted occasionally receiving hospitality from Native people along the way: "We passed through the woods and sometimes we lay in the woods by a fire and sometimes at Indians' houses or cabins" (Ni:618–619).

This epistle is a call to preach the gospel—whether to European settlers or Native Americans—and includes a sermon that begins in the universal spirit of Romans 1:20, and concludes with an invitation to live in peace through Christ. For Fox, the call to "answer the witness of God" applied equally to non-Christian and nominal-Christian. All need to be turned to the power of God within.

Scripture

As the hart panteth after the water brooks,
so panteth my soul after thee, O God.
My soul thirsteth for God, for the living God:
when shall I come and appear before God?
Psalms 42:1–2 (KJV)

Epistle

Dear friends,—

Be faithful in the power of the Lord God, . . . that you may answer the witness of God in every man, whether they . . . do not profess Christ, or whether they are such as do profess Christ, that have the form of godliness, and are out of the power. . . .

So as any are moved . . . in the power and love of God, to preach the gospel, (which is the love of God to them,) . . .

He is the living God
that clothes the earth with grass and herbs,
and causes the trees to grow,
and bring forth food for you,
and makes the fishes of the sea to breathe and live,
and makes the fowls of the air to breed,
and causes the roe and the hind, and the creatures,
and all the beasts of the earth to bring forth,
whereby they may be food for you.

He is the living God,
that causes the stars to arise in the night,
to give you light,
and the moon to arise
to be a light in the night.

He is the living God,
that causes the sun to give warmth unto you,
to nourish you when you are cold.

He is the living God,
that causes the snow and frost to melt,
and causes the rain to water the plants.

He is the living God,
that made the heaven and the earth, and the clouds,
and causes the springs to break out of the rocks,
and divided the great sea from the earth,
and divided the light from the darkness,
by which it is called day, and the darkness night,
and divided the great waters from the earth,
and gathered them together:
which great waters he called sea, and the dry land earth:
he is to be worshipped that doth this.

He is the living God,
that gives unto you breath, and life, and strength,
and gives unto you beasts and cattle,
whereby you may be fed and clothed.

He is the living God, . . .
and would have you . . . worship him in spirit,
and serve him who is holy and righteous,
and to live in peace;

who hath promised he will give Christ Jesus
for a covenant of light and peace to you. . . .

And now is the day approaching to you,
this covenant of light,
by which you shall come to have peace
with the Lord God, the king of the whole earth.

This is the King of kings, and Lord of lords,
in whose hand is the breath of all mankind:

this is the God of the spirits of all flesh,
who hath made all nations of mankind of one blood,
to dwell upon the face of the earth.

And . . . the sons and daughters of Adam, . . .
being in the transgression and sin,
led away with the god of the world, . . .
who causes people to destroy one another,
and murder one another about earthly things. . . .

And Christ, the second Adam,
the Lord from heaven, saves men from sin;

> who is the prince of peace, and of life,
> and the covenant of God,
>
> who brings men to have peace with God,
> and one with another,
>
> who destroys the devil,
> the author of strife:

this is Christ the second Adam,
which brings the sons and daughters of Adam
into reconciliation with God again,
and destroys sin, and finishes it,
and makes reconciliation
    for sin and iniquity.

The Victory of the Lamb Who Was Slain

These shall make war with the Lamb,
and the Lamb shall overcome them:
for he is Lord of lords, and King of kings:
and they that are with him
are called, and chosen, and faithful.
Revelation 17:14 (KJV)

Worthy is the Lamb that was slain to receive power,
and riches, and wisdom, and strength,
and honour, and glory, and blessing.
Revelation 5:12 (KJV)

The Mighty Day of the Lord (Epistle 38, 1653)

Introductory Note

Fox celebrates the coming Day of the Lord in the prophetic tradition of expectation that God will "burn up" evil and establish the comfortable rule of the saints. The original title was, *An Epistle to the travellers in the Lord's way, with a Testimony against the false prophets, and those that hold them up*. The testimony against the "false prophets, and those that hold them up," comes in the section with the repeated, "who are . . . ?" This is a polemic against paid clergy and their aristocratic sponsors.

Scripture

For the day of the Lord of hosts *shall be* upon every
one that is proud and lofty, and upon every one that
is lifted up; and he shall be brought low.
Isaiah 2:12 (KJV)

And every one that hath forsaken houses, or brethren, or sisters, or father, or mother, or wife, or children, or lands, for my name's sake, shall receive an hundredfold, and shall inherit everlasting life.
Matthew 19:29 (KJV)

Epistle

Friends,—

All are to receive your spiritual bread and water
from the Father of life,
by which ye may be strengthened and watered
from the Father of life,

in your passing and travelling on in your spiritual journey
heartily and comfortably;
that ye may come to your heavenly rest, . . .
the city of heavenly Jerusalem,
where ye shall abide eternally for ever.

Reason not with flesh and blood. . . .
But every one wait in the pure spirit to guide you to God,
then ye shall see the promise of God fulfilled in you,
and the springs of life opened to you,
and refreshment daily coming in from the Lord;

and then ye will come to walk with the Lord,
forsaking all,
father, mother, wife, and children, lands, livings,
and all. . . .

All honour, and glory, and thanks be to him for ever,
who now is come to rule alone in his saints.
Rejoice, O all ye prophets and righteous ones!

The beast, which made war with the lamb and the saints,
the lamb hath got the victory over the beast. . . .

Powerful Father and eternal God,
to thee alone be all glory, honour, and thanks for ever. . . .

Now all people, take notice!
who are they, that bear rule by their means?
Who are the hirelings now, that the scriptures speak of?
Who seek for their gain from their quarters now?
Who feed themselves with the fat now?
Who seek for the fleece, and clothe themselves with the wool now,
and so make a prey of the people? . . .
Where are the covetous teachers now?
Who are called of men master now?
Who love the chiefest places of the assemblies now?
Who go in long robes now? . . .
Who stone and stock, prison and beat now,
and hale before magistrates?. . . .

But the eternal, glorious God of heaven and earth,
the same as ever he was,
is manifesting himself in his sons and daughters,
who are called out of that generation and worship. . . .
The mighty day of the Lord is coming,
that shall burn as an oven. . . .

The Lord God of power will reign.
O happy day! praises! praises!
Praise ye the Lord, ye righteous ones;
sing praises to the Lord God Almighty for ever!. . . .

[H]e is risen and come in his saints,
who is Lord and king,
who will reign over all the world,
and bear the government upon his shoulders.

For the Lord is king in his saints,
he guards them, and guides them with his mighty power . . .
All glory and praise be to the Lord God Almighty for ever!

You That Have Come to the End (Epistle 239, 1664)

Introductory Note

In this epistle, originally titled, *A General Epistle to all Friends*, Fox demonstrates a new way to read the Book of Revelation. In fact, Fox does not read Revelation so much as he inhabits it. Instead of a coded chronology of the ultimate destruction of the world, Fox finds a description of spiritual and social realities already well known in the experience of the children of Light. The epistle begins with an exhortation to "be married and joined to the seed Christ the Lamb" for "by this you come to the end of the world." This is to say that those who have been searched and transformed by the Light and brought into union with Christ have overcome that which had separated them from God. They enter into the joyful fellowship of the new Jerusalem. This is the end of the power which "the world" had had in their lives, and in another sense, it is the in-breaking of eternal life into the life of the world.

Fox is well aware that the joy of dwelling with God is concurrent with the ongoing war of the Lamb. In England, in 1664, that is experienced as the nonviolent struggle against the entwined powers of false church and the oppressive state. These appear in the Revelation as "the whore" and "the beast/dragon," best recognized as the national churches which use the power of the state to enforce their false worship. The faithful follow the Lamb in suffering, but the promise is that they overcome "by the blood of the Lamb, and by the word of their testimony" (Revelation 12:11, KJV). The weapons of their warfare are spiritual, "not carnal."

Today, "the whore," "the dragon," and "the beast" reveal themselves in different forms than in seventeenth-century England. But those same entwined powers of concentrated wealth, propaganda, and violence used to compel conformity, are active in our day and are bringing about truly apocalyptic destruction. The "called and chosen"must bear testimony to the radically counter-cultural life of Jesus, as we experience the joy of the fellowship with each other. In these ways, eternity breaks into our ordinary time, the power of darkness yields to light, and we, too, have come to the end.

Note: I have added the scripture citations in brackets to demonstrate Fox's non-linear but liberating approach to the Revelation of John.

Scripture

These shall make war with the Lamb,
and the Lamb shall overcome them . . . and they that
are with him are called, and chosen, and faithful
Revelation 17:14 (KJV)

Epistle

All my dear friends and brethren, who are of the royal seed of God! . . .

be married and joined to the seed Christ the Lamb
[Rev 19:7]. . . .
For as you are joined to the seed,
and married to that which hath been slain
from the foundation of the world [Rev 13:7–8],
which hath the victory and doth overcome [Rev 17:14];
by this you come to the end of the world;
mark, to its end. . . .

And consider

how the witness hath been slain [Rev 20:4],

and (the true church,) the woman fled into the wilderness [Rev 12:6]; . . .

and how since that time the beast [Rev 13:12f; 14:9f] and dragon's worship hath been up, [Rev 13:4] . . . and the whore [Rev 17:1f; 19:2f], (the false church [Rev 17:18]) which hath ridden on the beast in the dragon's power [Rev 17:3],
whom the people have worshiped [Rev 13:8];

who hath caused all nations to drink of the whore's cup of fornication [Rev 14:8].

Now you that have come to the end,

and beyond all the worships of the beast, and after the worship of the dragon, [Rev 13:4; 19:20] . . .

and come to see the power, and to be in it, that takes them and casts them alive into the lake of fire [Rev 20:10f]; . . .

which power gives . . . to see to the very apostles' days [Rev 18:20], . . .

and what hath got up since then; for it is sixteen hundred years since the false prophets and Antichrists came in [Mark 13:22], (therefore they may plead antiquity.)

Now with the power of God ye may look . . . since the primitive times in the apostasy:

but now is the bride coming up out of the wilderness [Rev 21:2, 9],

and the prophet is arisen and arising [Rev 18:20],

and the everlasting gospel . . . is preached again to all nations, kindreds, tongues, and peoples, of them that dwell upon the earth [Rev 14:6–8];

and the reapers are going forth to reap people down, and so up to God, and to bring them into the barn, and to gather the wheat into the garner [Rev 14:16ff; Mat 13:30].

And people shall come to worship God, that made heaven and earth, the sea, and all that is therein [Rev 14:7],

and the beast's worship, and dragon's worship, and the great whore's church is falling [Rev 18:2ff],

the true woman is coming up [Rev 12:1f; 21:2],

false prophets are falling, true prophets and true witnesses are rising and risen [Rev 19:20].

Sing, triumph, and rejoice [Rev 19:1];
glory in the highest!

> trample, tread, and bow them
> before the mighty God:
> let the wicked bow
> before the gates of the righteous.

Sing and rejoice,
the heaven of heavens praise the Lord!

> Now the dragon's worship,
> beast, false church, false prophet are taken,
> the old dragon cast into the lake of fire,
> (and with him the false prophets,)
> and the flesh of the whore burnt.

Reap out, reap out, reap out, I say,
(with the power of God,)
ye reapers unto the Lord,
for here is the day of harvest [Rev 14:15]. . . .

The beginning of this ravening into this state was a matter of sixteen hundred years since, amongst whom is found the blood of the martyrs, . . . shed in this dark night of apostasy . . . with all their compelling worships, inventions, laws, traditions, churches, rudiments to be observed, and cups for people to drink.

In these, I say, and among these have the righteous suffered since the days of the apostles . . . and from amongst them will God fetch his royal seed with his own hand. . . .

Glory over all to him!
rejoice and sing praises,
he is now triumphing gloriously [Exo 15:1f; Rev 15:3],
  and bringing you over with his power. . . .

for the seed Christ is the first and the last, the beginning and the ending; and in the seed is the stayedness and plainness of words and life, yet a mystery to all them that be out of it. . . .

So the measuring line of righteousness [Isa 28:17] is in this known;

and also the state now wherein the Lamb and the saints shall have the victory [Rev 17:14];

and the rising of the witnesses, and the prophets, and the reapers going forth to reap the earth, [Rev 14:6–8,16–20]

and the woman is coming out of the wilderness, and the worshiping of God that made heaven and earth, the sea and the dry land is known [Rev 10:5–6; Gen 1:10];

and the destruction of the devil's worship, and the dragon's, and the false prophets, and the great whore, (the false church,)

and the saints shall reign, and the lamb shall have victory [Dan 7:21–22; Rev 17:14];

and the bride, the lamb's wife, shall be known, which is the true church, which Christ is the head of [Rev 21:9–10; Col 1:18]. . . .

So in the power of the Lord God meet, wait, live, and dwell, and have fellowship; for . . . in this power of God you will feel before the fall of Adam and Eve, where all things were good and blessed in the beginning before the fall; . . . so you that feel the redemption out of the fall, you know the state of the blessing before the fall, how all things were good and blessed:

come into the same power
that brings you up before the fall,
and brings you to be gathered
in the name of Jesus,
which is above every name,

and be gathered into the name of Jesus,
by which salvation is brought;
for there is no other name under heaven given,
by which salvation is brought,
but by the name of Jesus.

So, ye being gathered in the name
which is above every name,
and also in the name
by which salvation is brought,
and by no other name;

in that wait, and meet,
and keep together;
so ye will feel the blessing of the Lord
in you, and amongst you.

Concerning Spiritual Warfare (Epistle 55, 1653)

Introductory Note

In this epistle, *Concerning the Spiritual Warfare*, Fox calls forth a band of Quaker evangelists. Fox repeats the phrase, "Arm yourselves, like men of war," which divides the excerpt into two parts. In the first part, Fox urges Friends to "pity not" that which is evil for it should be attacked with "zeal." Elsewhere, Fox gives us this paradox: "Let mercy overshadow the judgment seat, and let mercy be mixed with judgment" (Epistle 263). The second part concerns the spiritual power ministers have to "answer that of God" and "lead out of prison" someone who has been bound by deceit. Can those who celebrate the universal love of God also condemn evil or oppression or degradation with zeal?

Scripture

Proclaim ye this among the Gentiles; Prepare war, wake up the mighty men, let all the men of war draw near; let them come up: Beat your plowshares into swords, and your pruninghooks into spears: let the weak say, I *am* strong.

Joel 3:9–10 (KJV)

Bring my soul out of prison, that I may praise thy name: the righteous shall compass me about; for thou shalt deal bountifully with me.
Psalm 142:7 (KJV)

Epistle

The word of the Lord God to all my brethren, babes, and soldiers, that are in the spiritual warfare of our Lord Jesus Christ.

[I.]
Arm yourselves, like men of war,
that ye may know what to stand against.

Spare not, pity not that which is for
the sword of the spirit,
plague, and famine,

and set up truth, and confound the deceit,
which stains the earth,
and cumbers the ground.

The dead stinks upon the earth,
and with it the earth is stained,
therefore bury it.

And wait in the light which comes from Jesus,
to be clothed with his zeal,
to stand against all them
who act contrary to the light. . . .

[II.]
Arm yourselves like men of war;

the mighty power of God goes along with you,
to enable you to stand over all the world,
and spiritually to chain, to fetter, to bind,

and to imprison, and to lead out of prison;
to famish, to feed, and to make fat,
and to bring into green pastures. . . .

And all waiting and walking in the light,
with it ye will see the Lord Jesus amongst you. . . .

And to you this is the word of the Lord.

Join to the Suffering Seed (Epistle 101, 1655)

Introductory Note

The original title of this epistle, *An exhortation to patience in the time of suffering*, lets us know that Fox was writing as one of many who had been imprisoned and fined for his faith. To be faithful, we must join Christ, "the suffering seed," because it is "the Lamb and not the rough nature" who "must have the victory." The rejection of violence of all sorts is the only way to be true to God, whose nature (and ultimate victory) is revealed to us in and by the Lamb of God.

Scripture

And I beheld, and I heard the voice of many angels round about the throne and the beasts and the elders: and the number of them was ten thousand times ten thousand, and thousands of thousands; Saying with a loud voice, Worthy is the Lamb that was slain to receive power, and riches, and wisdom, and strength, and honour, and glory, and blessing.

Revelation 5:11–12 (KJV)

Epistle

Dear Friends, . . .

be ready to offer up yourselves
in the power of God,
joining to the suffering seed,

in which ye offer up yourselves to God
in the patience,
in your sufferings,

feeling the seed
which was before that was
which makes to suffer.

For the lamb must have the victory,
mark, the lamb, and not the rough nature
which hath gotten up since man fell from God's image;
the lamb must have the victory over that.

So, give up all in the lamb's nature,
that in that ye may all meet
in life, in power, in victory, and dominion
over all that which is in the fall. . . .

In the Mighty Power of God Go On (Epistle 114, 1656)

Introductory Note

The epistle excerpted here is addressed to "E.B. and F.H." According to T. Canby Jones (Jones:90), E.B. and F.H. are Edward Burrough and Francis Howgill, members of the group of evangelists that came to be known as the "Valiant Sixty" who went out two-by-two from Swarthmoor Hall in the Northwest to all parts of England and abroad. Edward Burrough was thrown out of his home at age eighteen for his Quaker beliefs and teamed up with the older farmer, Francis Howgill.

Together, they were extremely effective preachers of the "mighty day of the Lord"—the time when God would enter human affairs to bring down the high, raise up the meek, and establish justice. Fox's five-fold exhortation to "go on" introduces the five sections into which I have divided this excerpt. Here are possible key words and themes for each section:

I. Dwell. The minister must first "dwell in the life of God."

II. Preach. Boldly declare the day of Lord.

III. Gather. Thresh out deceit and bring people "into the barn."

IV. Heal. There is power for healing.

V. Unity. Unity is found where Christ is the head.

Note: In section III, Fox uses the phrase, "the harlot's spirit." This language is found in the Book of Revelation, borrowed from the prophet Isaiah (Isaiah 1:21; Revelation 17:5–6; 19:2). In contrast to the "woman clothed in sun" (Revelation 12:1–16), the harlot is a symbol of the false church that provides legitimacy to oppressive political and economic power. It is worth considering what institutions today deceitfully legitimize extreme concentrations of wealth and violent power.

Scripture

For the day of the LORD of hosts *shall be* upon every
one that is proud and lofty, and upon every *one that*
is lifted up; and he shall be brought low.
Isaiah 2:12 (KJV)

Let both grow together until the harvest: and in the time of harvest
I will say to the reapers, Gather ye together first the tares, and bind
them in bundles to burn them: but gather the wheat into my barn.
Matthew 13:30 (KJV)

And as ye go, preach, saying, The kingdom of heaven is
at hand. Heal the sick, cleanse the lepers, raise the dead,
cast out devils: freely ye have received, freely give.
Matthew 10:7–8 (KJV)

Epistle

Dear brethren,

[I.]

in the mighty power of God go on,
to which power of the God of heaven and earth,
all the powers of the earth must bow;

that to that of God in all consciences
ye may be made manifest,
that that in them which is of God
may witness that ye are sent of God.

Dwell in the life of God,
that to the spirits in prison ye may minister
and to [them] be made manifest,
that ye are no deceivers, but saviours,
and such as are sent to lead from all deceivers,
and to testify against them.

[II.]

So, in the mighty power of the Lord go on,
preaching the gospel to every creature,
and disciplining them
in the name of the Father, son, and holy spirit.

In the name of Christ
preach the mighty day of the Lord
to all the consciences of them
who have lain long in darkness,
and under its chain,
where the light shined,
but the darkness could not comprehend it.

[III.]

So, in the power of the Lord God go on,
and thresh that which hath been fed with the harlot's spirit,

and the harlot famish,
which hath and doth prison the just.

I charge you in the presence of the living God,
dwell in his power,
that with his power
ye may be carried along to minister
to all the spirits imprisoned by the deceit.

As the life of God doth arise,
it will lead you up to God, the Father of life;
in this your fruits shall never wither.

But go on to plant a vineyard,
and to plough,
that ye may eat the fruit thereof;

and to plant in hope,
and to thresh in hope,
that ye may be made partakers of your hope.

And to thresh out the corn,
that the wind may scatter the chaff,
that the corn may be gathered into the barn.

[IV.]

So, in the power of the Lord Jesus Christ
preach the everlasting gospel,
that by his power
the sick may be healed,
the leprous cleansed,
the dead raised,
the blind eyes opened,
and the devils cast out.

[V.]

In the name of the Lord Jesus Christ go on,
that that of God in all consciences may witness,
that ye are sent of God, and are of God;

and so according to that speak,
to bring up all unto the head Christ,
and into the life which gave forth the scriptures;

for there is the unity,
and out of it is the confusion.

Walk Cheerfully—To Friends in the Ministry (*Journal*, for 1656)

Introductory Note

Famous among Friends for the expression, "you will come to walk cheerfully over the world answering that of God in everyone," this epistle is the most complete presentation of Fox's view of public ministry. It is essential that the ministers have first known the transforming power of God in their own lives. Sound doctrine and argument have a place in public ministry, as the Spirit leads, but the only ministry that can free someone who has long been "in prison" to deceit, is a divine power secretly operating in the life of the minister. It is only when we dwell in the power of God that we will "*then* come to walk cheerfully . . . answering that of God in everyone" (my emphasis).

Fox closes with an exhortation to be valiant in the Lamb's war. Ministers are to "spare no deceit" and "keep . . . clear of the blood of all men." This draws on the parable of the watchman in Ezekiel 33:1–9. The watchman who fails to warn against coming danger is responsible for "the blood" of those who were not warned. This leads into a call to righteousness where we get a strong taste of Fox's preaching.

Because it is included in Fox's *Journal*, we know that the letter was written from Launceston Jail in 1656. Fox had been arrested with some companions near Lands End in Cornwall for distributing "several papers tending to the disturbance of the public peace" and for not having a pass for his travels and for refusing to swear the Oath of Abjuration of 1655 (Ni: 247). They were imprisoned at Launceston Castle, January 22 to

September 9, 1656, including thirteen days in the truly vile Doomsdale dungeon (Ni:242–266).

Here is the full text of Fox's Letter to Friends in the Ministry (*Works* 1:287–289). An abridgment is in Ni:263–264. Angle brackets <enclose> text that is not in Nickalls but is in the *Works*. The Rufus Jones edition of the *Journal of George Fox* does not include this letter.

Scripture

Sow to yourselves in righteousness, reap in mercy; break
up your fallow ground: for *it is* time to seek the LORD,
till he come and rain righteousness upon you.
Hosea 10:12 (KJV)

But if the watchman see the sword come, and blow not the
trumpet, and the people be not warned; if the sword come,
and take any person from among them, he is taken away in his
iniquity; but his blood will I require at the watchman's hand.
Ezekiel 33:6 (KJV)

Epistle

[Introduction and summary.]

About this time I was moved to give forth the following exhortation to Friends in the ministry:

Friends, In the power of life and wisdom, and dread of the Lord God of life, and heaven and earth, dwell; that in the wisdom of God over all ye may be preserved, and be a terror to all the adversaries of God, and a dread, answering that of God in them all, spreading the truth abroad, awakening the witness, confounding the deceit, gathering up out of transgression into the life, the covenant of light and peace with God.

Let all nations hear the sound by word or writing.
Spare no place, spare no tongue, nor pen;
but be obedient to the Lord God:

go through the work;
be valiant for the truth upon earth;
tread and trample upon all that is contrary.

[The Spiritual Condition of the Minister.]

<Ye have the power, do not abuse it;
and strength and presence of the Lord;
eye it, and the wisdom;
that with it you may all be ordered
to the glory of the Lord God.

Keep in the dominion;
keep in the power over all deceit;
tread over them in that which lets you see to the world's end,
and the utmost parts of the earth.

Reign and rule with Christ,
whose sceptre and throne are now set up,
whose dominion is over all
to the ends of the earth;

whose dominion is an everlasting dominion,
his throne an everlasting throne,
his kingdom an everlasting kingdom,
his power above all powers.

Therefore this is the word of the Lord to you all,>

Keep in the wisdom of God,
that spreads over all the earth;
the wisdom of the creation,
that is pure from above, not destructive.

For now shall salvation go out of Zion,
to judge the mount of Esau;

now shall the law go forth from Jerusalem,
to answer the principle of God in all;
to hew down all inventors and inventions.

For all the princes of the earth are but as air
to the power of the Lord God,
which you are in,
and have tasted of;
therefore live in it,

that is the word of the Lord God to you all;
do not abuse it;
keep down and low;
and take heed of false joys,
that will change.

[The Process of Ministry.]

Bring all into the worship of God.
Plough up the fallow ground.
<Thresh and get out the corn;

that the seed, the wheat, may be gathered into the barn:
that to the beginning all people may come;
to Christ, who was before the world was made.

For the chaff is come upon the wheat by transgression.
He that treads it out is out of transgression,
fathoms transgression,

puts a difference between the precious and the vile,
can pick out the wheat from the tares,
and gather into the garner;

so brings to the lively hope the immortal soul,
into God out of which it came.

None worship God
but who come to the principle of God,
which they have transgressed.>

None are ploughed up
but he who comes to the principle of God in him,
that he hath transgressed.

Then he doth service to God;
then is the planting, watering,
and increase from God.

So the ministers of the spirit
must minister to the spirit that is in prison,
which hath been in captivity in every one;

that with the spirit of Christ
people may be led out of captivity up to God,
the Father of spirits, to serve him,
and have unity with him,
with the scriptures, and one with another.

This is the word of the Lord God to you all, a charge to you all in the presence of the living God;

be patterns, be examples
in all countries, places, islands, nations,
wherever you come;

that your life and conduct
may preach among all sorts of people,
and to them.

Then you will come to walk cheerfully over the world,
answering that of God in every one;
whereby in them ye may be a blessing,
and make the witness of God in them to bless you:

then to the Lord God
you shall be a sweet savour,
and a blessing.

[Exhortation To Be Valiant.]

Spare no deceit. Lay the sword upon it; go over it.
Keep yourselves clear of the blood of all men,
either by word or writing,

and keep yourselves clean,
<that you may stand in your throne,
and every one have his lot
and stand in the lot in the ancient of days.

The blessing of the Lord be with you,
and keep you over all the idolatrous worships and worshippers.
Let them know the living God;

for teachings, churches, worships
must be thrown down
with the power of the Lord God,
set up by man's earthly understanding, knowledge, and will.
All this must be thrown down
with that which gave forth the scripture;
and who are in that, reign over it all.

That is the word of the Lord God to you all.

In that is God worshipped,
that brings to declare his will,
and brings to the church in God,
the ground and pillar of truth:

for now is the mighty day of the Lord appeared,
and the arrows of the Almighty gone forth;
which shall stick in the hearts of the wicked.

Now will I arise, saith the Lord God Almighty,
to trample and thunder down deceit,
which hath long reigned and stained the earth.

Now will I have my glory out of every one.

The Lord God Almighty over all in his strength and power keep you to his glory, that you may come to answer that of God in every one in the world.

Proclaim the mighty day of the Lord of fire and sword,
who will be worshipped in spirit and in truth,

and keep in the life and power of the Lord God,
that the inhabitants of the earth may tremble before you:
that God's power and majesty may be admired
among hypocrites and heathen,

and ye in the wisdom, dread, life, terror, and dominion
preserved to his glory;>
that nothing may rule or reign but power and life itself,
and in the wisdom of God ye may be preserved in it.

< This is the word of the Lord God to you all.

The call is now
out of transgression,
the spirit bids, come.

The call is now
from all false worships and gods,
from all inventions and dead works,
to serve the living God.

The call is to repentance,
to amendment of life,
whereby righteousness may be brought forth,
which shall go throughout the earth.

Therefore ye that be chosen and faithful,
who are with the Lamb,
go through your work faithfully
in the strength and power of the Lord,

and be obedient to the power;
for that will save you out of the hands of unreasonable men,
and preserve you over the world to himself.

Hereby you may live in the kingdom
    that stands in power,
    which hath no end;
    where glory and life is. >

Sing, Ye Witnesses for the King of Saints (Epistle 138, 1657)

Introductory Note

This beautiful song of encouragement is addressed *To the Prisoners*, i.e., to Friends who have been imprisoned for their faith. Rich with the language of Revelation, Fox assures them that, although they are "in outward bonds," they have the victory because "you are not your own."

Scripture

What? know ye not that . . . ye are not your
own? For ye are bought with a price.
1 Corinthians 6:19–20 (KJV)

And I saw as it were a sea of glass mingled with fire: and them that had gotten the victory over the beast, . . . stand on the sea of glass, having the harps of God. And they sing . . . the song of the Lamb, saying, Great and marvellous *are* thy works, Lord God Almighty; just and true *are* thy ways, thou King of saints.
Revelation 15:2–3 (KJV)

Epistle

Friends,—

Ye that are the prisoners
of the Lord Jesus Christ
in outward bonds,

who witness him
by whom the world was made,
who is the King of saints,
and who are his,
        and come under his dominion
        and government,

ye are not your own;
but purchased with his blood,
        which washes and makes you clean, and justifies,
        whose bodies are his temple.

Though he suffers you to be imprisoned,
yet in his power your bodies are kept,
and your spirits also;

ye standing witnesses
        for your master,
        for your king,
        for your prophet,
        for your covenant of light,
        for your wisdom of God,
                him by whom all things were made,
        for the word and power,
                by which all things were made and upheld,

        against the powers of darkness,
                who are out of the light,
                out of the truth,

who cannot bind, stop nor limit
the unlimited power,
which is over it,
and comprehends it.

They who are born of the word,
and in the power which upholds all things,
over that, and the power of the evil one,
have victory,
and sing
over the false prophet. . . .

and there is the beast,
that makes the war
against the lamb and his saints,
who witness the testimony of Jesus,
and the word of God.

Therefore

mind the word of God,
ye children of the light,
who are in the light,
that comes from the word;

mind the word of the Lord, which is
as a hammer,
and as a fire,
and sharper than a two-edged sword.

And ye who are the Lord's,
are not your own. . . .

The Church in Her Glory Appearing (Epistle 169, 1658)

Introductory Note

The importance of this message to Fox is underlined by the appended note: *This is to go to all the meetings of Friends among them to be read. London, the 11 th of the 3 d month, 1658.* Fox opens by greeting "the elect, chosen and faithful" and acknowledging that Friends are enduring confiscation of goods, imprisonment, whipping, mocking, "and some have been tried unto death." After a beautiful affirmation of the suffering church, Fox numbered paragraphs 2–6; these contain instruction, which can be summarized: be obedient to God's leadings, do not quench the spirit, guard the fellowship.

Note, in paragraph three: the phrases "to reprove sin in the gate" and "to exhort high or low" refers to prophetic condemnation of social injustice by those Friends led by the Spirit into ministry in public places.

Scripture

Moreover I will make a covenant of peace with them; it shall be an everlasting covenant with them: and I will place them, and multiply them, and will set my sanctuary in the midst of them for evermore.
Ezekiel 37:26 (KJV)

Because of the savour of thy good ointments thy name is as ointment poured forth, therefore do the virgins love thee.
Song of Solomon 1:3 (KJV)

Epistle

To all the elect, chosen and faithful,

who are of the royal seed of God,
living stones, elect and precious,

knit and built up together, and united,
the family and household of God,

and come to his mountain,
that is established upon the top of all mountains,
that walk in the light of the Lord,
in unity and covenant with God,
in the covenant of life and peace with him.

Who in this the Lamb's day are the gold tried in the fire.

Who have been tried
by goods spoiling,
by bonds, by whippings,
by mockings, and reproaches
in the day of the Lamb's power,

and some have been tried unto death;
and ye have proved to be the pure gold,
that hath come out brighter and brighter.

Who have not feared the waves of the sea, nor the winds;
who fear not the storms nor the weather;

whose anchor holds,
which is the hope, the mystery,
which anchors the soul which is immortal,
to the immortal God.

Among whom the star of Jacob is seen,
and the morning star is risen,
and the sun of righteousness shines,
and the Lamb's voice is known,

the church in her glory and beauty
is appeared and appearing;
the marriage of the lamb, and the bride,
and the wedding day is known,
in which there is unity;

and the virgins sing praises,
and follow the Lamb, because of his sweet ointment;
and the virgins are upon Mount Zion.

And the gospel is going forth
unto all nations, kindreds, and tongues;
and life and immortality are coming to light
through the gospel, which is the power of God;

and the mystery of the fellowship is known,
which is in the power. . . .

2. And now, friends, if any be moved of the Lord God by his power, be obedient to it, and wait in the life and in the power, and it will direct you to the glory of God, in his wisdom, not to abuse it; that whatsoever ye do, ye may do it to his glory, ye answering the just principle of God in every one.

3. If any be moved to go to the steeple-houses, or markets, or to reprove sin in the gate, or to exhort high or low, or to reprove them; reason not with flesh and blood, nor quench the spirit. And when ye have done, in the same spirit live; and then ye will have peace, and rest, and fellowship with God, and one with another. For the unity is in the spirit, and it is the bond of peace.

4. And all Friends, in your meetings do not quench the spirit. And take heed, and do not judge one another in the meetings; but have patience until the meetings be done. So, if any have any thing upon him to speak to another, he may speak to him after the meeting is done; that will cover one another's weakness, and not hurt others.

5. And all Friends every where, wait to feel the power of God in yourselves in your meetings. And take heed of sleeping, and feel the power of God in one another. . . .

6. And Friends all every where, dwell in the love and fear of the Lord God, and in peace one with another, and in the power and life of the Lord God keep your meetings; and live in the mystery of the fellowship of the gospel, which is everlasting.

There Is a Summer Religion (Epistle 205, 1661)

Introductory Note

In the midst of calamitous events, it is helpful to be reminded of the power of God over evil and the love and life we have in Christ. Fox wrote this as the Commonwealth collapsed. With the reinstatement of the monarchy, the state church changed as well. The summer religion of the former Puritan state church cannot survive in the winter, when the former persecutors flee or renounce their faith. "But the religion that is in the power of God" (meaning the independent churches, such as Friends) is "the standing religion." In today's political and social turmoil, here is encouragement to find a standing religion in the love and power of God.

In the concluding stanzas of this epistle/psalm, Fox drums out the power of light over darkness, truth over falsehood. Fox closes with the lovely postscript, *From a lover of your souls, and your everlasting good*.

Scripture

For I am persuaded, that neither death, nor life, nor angels, nor
principalities, nor powers, nor things present, nor things to come,
Nor height, nor depth, nor any other creature, shall be able to
separate us from the love of God, which is in Christ Jesus our Lord.
Romans 8:38–39 (KJV)

Epistle

All Friends,

live in God's dominion, and power, and life,
which was before storms and tempests were,
in which ye may feel life
and dominion, power, and victory,

the Lord's power being lived in,
    which was before tempests were,
    in which ye will have the victory.

There is a summer religion,
    which appears when the sun shineth upon them;
and in the summer time all the venomous creatures
    creep out of their holes, corners, and dens,
    and the flies, wasps, and snakes;

but when the winter is come,
    and the storms and tempests come,
    then the summer religion is gone,
then the venomous, viperous creatures'
    religion and works are gone.

But the religion that is in the power of God standeth,
    which was before the devil was,
    and all his works and children.
And so that is the standing religion,
    that is in the power of God,
    which was before the power of darkness was.

And, friends, ye that know the light of Jesus Christ, and have tasted of his power, by which ye come to be gathered into the name of Jesus, do not forsake the assembling of yourselves together; but provoke one another, and exhort one another to love, and to good works,

and let not powers,
    nor principalities,
    nor prisons, thrones, nor dominions,
    spoiling your goods, mockings, scoffings,
    nor reproachings, and pluckers off your hair,
    and smiters,
separate you from the love of God,
that ye have in Christ Jesus,
who conquered death and the devil,

the power of it,
the adversary,
the wicked one,
the enmity.
Christ is the life, the light, the love of God to mankind . . .
the life that destroys death,
and the light which destroys darkness,
and the truth that destroys error and all falsehood,
and the power of God
that destroys the power of the devil,

and being gathered into Christ
and into his name,
keep your meetings in the power of God
and in his light and life,

whose gathering is above all other gatherings in the earth;
and Christ's name is above all other names on the earth.

And feel the seed of God
set over all that which makes to suffer;
which was before it was,
and will remain when it is gone. . . .

From a lover of your souls, and your everlasting good.

Armour of Light (Epistle 206, 1661)

Introductory Note

This excerpt from a much longer epistle speaks to the spiritual weapons wielded by the "children of Light" during the days of persecution. Could the kingdom of God be brought in by force of arms? Both Quakers and the Fifth Monarchy Men, found their conflicting answers to that question in a passage in Daniel chapter 2. Nebuchadnezzar has a dream in which four kingdoms are superseded by a fifth kingdom—

which is the kingdom of God. For Fox, the critical element missed by the Fifth Monarchy Men was that the kingdom of God was brought in by a "stone cut out of the mountain without hands." Friends took this to mean that the weapons of the kingdom of God were spiritual, not carnal. Wherever we feel the impulse to use violence to establish justice, the children of Light need to remember to "put on the armour of light" and seek to live by the power of God, not physical force.

Scripture

For the weapons of our warfare are not carnal, but mighty through God to the pulling down of strong holds.
2 Corinthians 10:4 (KJV)

Finally, my brethren, be strong in the Lord, and in the power of his might. Put on the whole armour of God, that ye may be able to stand against the wiles of the devil.
Ephesians 6:10–11 (KJV)

And in the days of these kings shall the God of heaven set up a kingdom, which shall never be destroyed: and the kingdom shall not be left to other people, but it shall break in pieces and consume all these kingdoms, and it shall stand for ever. Forasmuch as thou sawest that the stone was cut out of the mountain without hands, and that it brake in pieces the iron, the brass, the clay, the silver, and the gold; the great God hath made known to the king what shall come to pass hereafter: and the dream is certain, and the interpretation thereof sure.
Daniel 2:44–45 (KJV)

Epistle

In the power of God . . . remain, in this your day of trial . . . [I]n it is your peace and kingdom. And though ye have not a foot of ground to stand upon, yet ye have the power of God to skip and to leap in; standing in that which is your life, that is everlasting. . . .

So, put on the armour of light, that with it ye may be able to defend, and see, and walk, and stand against all the arrows and darts that are in the unrighteous world . . . as children of the light, and children of the day. . . .

Put on your breast-plate of righteousness . . . to keep you from all that which would defile and surfeit it, or cause you to be weary, or think the war or time long. . . .

Put on therefore the shield of faith, by which . . . ye have the victory. For faith is a mystery held in a pure conscience, by which ye have access to God. . . . In that faith be joyful. . . .

Put on the helmet of salvation, and take the sword of the spirit, (the word of God,) . . . Christ Jesus being your helmet and . . . the sword of the spirit that mortifies, that crucifies, baptizes, cuts off . . . all corruptions that have gotten up since the transgression; then in the spirit ye will worship God, and have . . . spiritual weapons, and come to be spiritual men, and not as the carnal world that rule and wrestle with carnal weapons, and with flesh and blood.

The stone cut out of the mountain without hands,
will dash and break into pieces
all the cutters with hands,
and carnal-weaponed men
about religion, church, and worship;
and his kingdom is an everlasting kingdom,
and his dominion hath no end.

This stone
is that which laid Nebuchadnezzar's head low,
and brought him to eat grass like a beast;
who knew not the kingdom of the Most High
ruling in men.

So ye that know this stone
cut out of the mountain without hands,
ye all know the kingdom of the most high God
ruling in you,

and his dominion which is everlasting,
and come to be his temple.

For there was but one temple in the whole world
commanded of God, as a figure of Christ,
who would dwell in man,
in male and female,
who should be the temples of God,
in whom should be
his name and power. . . .

So all dear lambs, and babes, and brethren,
happy and blessed are ye who know the seed,
which is heir of the blessings,
and the power, and life,
and the kingdom,
and the world that is everlasting
and without end.

Sing and Rejoice, Ye Children of the Day (Epistle 227, 1663)

Introductory Note

With Epistles 235 and 236, this is one of three great hymns of faith written by Fox in the face of persecution. Fox wrote this in *The 9 th month, 1663*. The persecution had taken the lives of several of the great leaders of the movement, including the beloved Friend, Edward Burrough, who died in February of 1663 from illness he contracted in prison.

Note the interesting two-part structure of the epistle: the first part celebrates the coming victory of the Lamb over all evil; the second part, finds life and peace "in the seed Christ," who brings us to a "life that was with the Father before the world began." The present time of persecution does not lie between these two realities but is simultaneously involved with both.

Scripture

Sing and rejoice, O daughter of Zion: for, lo, I come, and
I will dwell in the midst of thee, saith the LORD.
Zechariah 2:10 (KJV)

These are they which follow the Lamb whithersoever
he goeth. These were redeemed from among men,
being the firstfruits unto God and to the Lamb.
Revelation 14:4 (KJV)

Ye are all the children of light, and the children of the
day: we are not of the night, nor of darkness.
1 Thessalonians 5:5 (KJV)

And the LORD said unto Moses, Stretch out thine hand
toward heaven, that there may be darkness over the
land of Egypt, even darkness *which* may be felt.
Exodus 10:21 (KJV)

Epistle

[I.]
Sing and rejoice,
ye children of the day and of the light;
for the Lord is at work
in this thick night of darkness
that may be felt.

And truth doth flourish as the rose,
and the lilies do grow among the thorns,
and the plants atop of the hills,
and upon them the lambs do skip
and play.

And never heed the tempests
nor the storms, floods nor rains,
for the seed Christ is over all,
            and doth reign.

And so be of good faith and valiant for the truth:
for the truth can live in the jails.
And fear not the loss of the fleece,
for it will grow again;

and follow the lamb,
if it be under the beast's horns,
or under the beast's heels;
for the lamb shall have the victory
            over them all.

[II.]

And so all live in the seed Christ,
your way, that never fell;
and you do see over all the ways
of Adam's and Eve's sons and daughters
            in the fall.

And in the seed Christ, your way,
you have life and peace;
and there you do see
over all the ways of Adam in the fall,
            in which there is no peace.

So in the seed Christ stand and dwell,
in whom you have life and peace;
the life that was with the Father
            before the world began.

And the Rock Remaineth (Epistle 235, 1664)

Introductory Note

With Epistles 227 and 236, this is one of three great hymns of faith written by Fox in the face of persecution. Fox's imagery creates a "safe place" in this poetic meditation for the Friends who are suffering traumatic loss: "the rock remaineth, . . . so dwell in the love of God."

Note: At one point, Fox writes, "all sufficient, omnipotent God, *Elshdy*." The Hebrew is sometimes rendered *el shaddai* and is often translated "Almighty," as in Ezekiel 1:24, KJV. Some versions, like the Jewish Publication Society, TANAKH (1985), leave the word untranslated.

Note also: "Land flood" refers to an overflowing river, a common occurrence in England, particularly in the eastern fells, which were the subject of a major but unsuccessful drainage scheme in the seventeenth century. Whether Fox had a literal or figurative flood in mind is not known.

Scripture

> He is like a man which built an house, and digged deep,
> and laid the foundation on a rock: and when the flood
> arose, the stream beat vehemently upon that house, and
> could not shake it: for it was founded upon a rock.
> Luke 6:48 (KJV)

Epistle

Friends,—

You who now come to suffer by a land flood,

keep on the rock,
for there is safety,

though a storm be in the sea,
and the flood be great,
and the winds great,
and the way rough and crooked,
the seed Christ can make all plain.

And so think not the winter and cold weather,
nor the night, long;
for the lilies do grow,
and the gardens do give a good smell. . . .

And the sun shines,
and the light is clear, and not dim,
that you may see your way, and life,
though there is a storm and tempest in the sea. . . .

And the rock remaineth.

. . . And the Lord's eye is open, and he sees all the actions of men, and times and seasons are in his hands, who is King of kings and Lord of lords; the strong and all sufficient, omnipotent God, *Elshdy*, who destroyeth the destroyer. . . . And so . . .

keep your fellowship in the power of God,
and look above all outward sufferings,
and dwell in that which is above all,
and will stand when all other is gone.

And so dwell in the love of God,
and in the unity of the spirit,
one with another. . . . Amen.

In the Winds and Storms (Epistle 236, 1664)

Introductory Note

With Epistles 227 and 235, this epistle makes a triplet of psalms of comfort for suffering Friends during the years of persecution that followed the restoration of the monarchy. This epistle ends with a contest between the "cords of the ungodly" and "the cords of love, the power of God." It is worth reflecting on what cords bind and pull on us and on our communities.

Scripture

The kings of the earth set themselves,
and the rulers take counsel together,
against the LORD, and against his anointed, saying,
Let us break their bands asunder,
and cast away their cords from us.
He that sitteth in the heavens shall laugh:
the Lord shall have them in derision.
Psalm 2:2–4 (KJV)

Epistle

All my dear friends, in the everlasting power, life, and truth live, for you cannot live without it in the winds and storms.

And though the hills and the mountains are burned,
and the trees are become fruitless,
and winter hath devoured the former fruits,
    and you do see that persecution hath choked them,
    and the heat hath scorched them;

whereby the untimely figs are fallen,
and the corn is withered on the house-top,
    and the night is come,
    and the evil beasts go out of their den.

But truth lives,
    and the power of God is over them all;

and Christ ruleth,
        and there is bread of life,
        and water of life in him,

and in his house;
        though the caterpillars and locusts
        are agreed to eat up all the green.

But, as you are in the truth,
you are in its day;
        and they in the darkness,
        are in the day of darkness.

And all who are in the truth,
rejoice through Christ,
in the God of truth,

and never heed prisons,
for they are but for a time;
        and mind him who hath all times
        and seasons in his hand.

And never heed the raging waves of the sea,
nor be troubled at his tongue
that speaks nothing but tribulation,
anguish, and bondage;

nor be troubled at the cords of the ungodly;
        for the cords of love,
        the power of God
        are stronger.

And what doth he that sits in heaven,
but laugh them to scorn?

And so be valiant for the truth upon the earth,
for the power is the Lord's.

And so my love to all Friends in the everlasting seed, that never fell nor changeth.

Only the Living Word Produces Authentic Ministry (Epistle 249, 1667)

Introductory Note

All Christians are ministers. Only one condition applies, namely that gospel ministry rises from "God's word in your hearts. . . ." These excerpts from a much longer epistle titled, *A general epistle to Friends, and all people, to read over and consider in the fear of God*, reveal Fox's passionate identification with working-class people. Rich, poor, male, female: all need the living Word of God within for authentic ministry. Fox's sense of humor must have had his hearers laughing along with his imagined dialog as he confounds church authorities.

Note: In the argument about "original" languages of the scriptures (Hebrew and Greek), the term, "a divine" or "divines," refers to theologians and ordained clergy.

Scripture

Thy word *is* a lamp unto my feet, and a light unto my path.
Psalm 119:105 (KJV)

For the word of God *is* quick, and powerful, and sharper
than any twoedged sword, piercing even to the dividing
asunder of soul and spirit, and of the joints and marrow, and
is a discerner of the thoughts and intents of the heart.
Hebrews 4:12 (KJV)

And it shall come to pass in the last days, saith God,
I will pour out of my Spirit upon all flesh.
Acts 2:17 (KJV)

Epistle

[The Word is a Light that Empowers Ministry.]

. . . . [A]ll are to learn of Christ, the light, the life, and the truth, . . . And mind every one God's word in your hearts, and in your mouths, and obey it. . . .

> Therefore . . . take David's lamp and light.
> You may say, what is that? and where is it?
> I say it is with you, the word of God . . .
>
> You may say, people do not use to carry lamps
> in the day-time, but in the night.
> I say, you are in the night of darkness,
> and therefore the word is called a lamp,
> and a light to you;
>
> by which you may see
> the way of the Lord, which is perfect,
> from all men's ways, which are imperfect;
>
> by which ye may see
> the path of the just to be a shining light,
> from all the unjust paths that are in the darkness.
>
> For by this word
> did David . . . spake so many glorious expressions,
> which the world since hath turned into metre,
> and made songs of them.
>
> And this was the word
> that came to Abraham . . .
> And . . . to Jacob, the shepherd . . .
> And . . . to Moses, the shepherd . . .
> And Elisha, the ploughman . . .
> And . . . Amos the herdsman . . .
>
> And this was the word
> that made so many fishermen

preachers of the gospel,
which is the power of God.

And this was the word which made
Matthew the toll gatherer,
Luke the physician,
and Paul the tent maker,
ministers and preachers of the gospel, and power of God.

And this was the word
which made Peter to see Joel's prophecy,
how that God would pour out of his spirit upon all flesh,
and sons and daughters should prophesy,
and young men should see visions,
and old men dream dreams;

and the pouring forth of the spirit
upon servants and handmaids,
that every one should have something to speak
to the glory of God.

[Controversy: What Qualifies a Person for Ministry?]

And now priests, and proud prelates, and bishops, and popes, though you have made a trade of the saints' words, and apostles' and prophets' words, and gotten a great deal of money by them, (which were fishermen and shepherds' words from the word,) yet nevertheless, if a company of shepherds, herdsmen, fishermen, tent makers and toll gatherers should come amongst you to preach, you would say, Away with these mechanic fellows, they have not served seven years apprenticeship at the colleges, which were set up to make ministers; therefore they are not to set up, because they have not served their apprenticeship.

What say the shepherds, herdsmen, fishermen, tent makers, physicians, and toll gatherers? Do you make a trade of our friends' words, who were of our occupation, that never served apprenticeships in colleges, before they spake forth the words you make a trade of?

What! will you make a trade of our friends' words, who were of our occupation? Away with you to work, and away with your colleges; for our brother Paul the tent maker said, he that will not work must not eat.

For, would you own Christ if he had come in your day, who was called, a carpenter's son? You popes, with your triple crowns, and you lord bishops, with your coaches and pampered horses, and gorgeous apparel, with your black coats, and white coats, and silk girdles: are you like to entertain him who was called a carpenter's son? Or to cast him and his mother into the manger in your stables?. . . .

The priests say that Hebrew, Greek, and Latin, are the original; but the many languages began at Babel. . . . And all the priests that have gotten the many languages, which began at Babel, they tell simple ignorant people that they have the original, and are the orthodox men, . . . and say, the Quakers are a simple people, and despise the learned orthodox men, who have the original.

Give ear O people! If these languages, which came up at the confounding of Babel, are the priests' original that makes them orthodox and divine, then Pilate, that crucified Christ, was as good an orthodox divine as they; for when he crucified Christ, he wrote a paper in Hebrew, Greek, and Latin, and set atop of him . . . and so then tongues neither are the original, nor make orthodox nor divine. . . . Now it is clear that the gospel must be preached to all nations and tongues; and that tongues are not the original, neither do they make divines, or orthodox men; but it is clear that it is the word which was in the beginning which makes a divine; yea, of tradesmen, who are base and contemptible in the eyes of the proud. . . .

And so we say, that the word of God is the original, which doth fulfill the scriptures; and

the word is it which makes a divine,
which is called a hammer,
but it is a living hammer;

and is called a sword and fire,
but it is a living sword,
and a living fire,

to hammer, and cut down, and burn up
that which separated
and kept man from God;

by which word
man is reconciled again to God,
which is called the word of reconciliation;

by this word
are men and women
sanctified and made clean. . . .

[The True Priesthood.]

[T]he Jew inward, he offers
in his temple the spiritual sacrifices;
and no where else doth he offer but in his temple;
for by the spirit, doth he offer to God,
who is a spirit. . . .

And they that offered in the Jews' temple,
were to wear the holy garments;
so are you to do that are the true christians,
and are called a royal priesthood.

[Q.] What! are all true christians priests?
[A.] Yes.

[Q.] What! are women priests?
[A.] Yes, women priests.

[Q.] And can men and women offer sacrifices without they wear the holy garments?
[A.] No.

[Q.] What are the holy garments men and women must wear?
[A.] The fine linen; and they must go in white. . . .

[Q.] What is the fine linen and going in white, that this royal priesthood must wear, which are the royal garments?
[A.] It is the righteousness of Christ, which is the righteousness of the saints . . . men and women. . . .

The kingdom of God stands in righteousness,
and faith, and joy in the holy ghost. . . .
Therefore love one another,
instead of persecuting one another;

and be meek, and not high;
and entreat, and not threaten;
and bless, and not curse;
and love, and not hate;
and do good, and not evil;

and live in the will of God,
  and be not self-willed;
and mind the religion of Christ,
  and not your own. . . .

All Come to the Flock of Christ (Epistle 270, 1669)

Introductory Note

Fox begins this epistle with an image of Friends as a flock enjoying the springs of life, but the phrase "and therefore" signals an important shift: these gifts are not for ourselves only. The epistle turns out to be a call to ministry, which fulfills our destiny as temples of Christ. Fox closes with the prayer that "the word of God . . . may have its passage through you all." This vividly underscores Fox's understanding that ministry is an offer to be, as far as possible, a transparent vessel for the divine Word to have "passage" into the world.

Scripture

If thou know not, O thou fairest among women, go thy way forth by the footsteps of the flock, and feed thy kids beside the shepherds' tents.
Song of Solomon 1:8 (KJV)

For God, who commanded the light to shine out of darkness, hath shined in our hearts, to *give* the light of the knowledge of the glory of God in the face of Jesus Christ.
2 Corinthians 4:6 (KJV)

We have also a more sure word of prophecy; whereunto ye do well that ye take heed, as unto a light that shineth in a dark place, until the day dawn, and the day star arise in your hearts.
2 Peter 1:19 (KJV)

Epistle

All that are gathered in the name of Jesus,
and are made alive by him
and quickened by him,
come to the flock of Christ;
and know where they feed at noon-day,

they are gathered into the name of Jesus Christ,
whose name is above every name;
and know that there is
no salvation under the whole heaven,
but in the name of Jesus, . . .

and see his pastures of life,
see his springs of life,
and his rivers of life,
and his bread of life;

and see the footsteps of the flock,
the testimony of Jesus, the spirit,
by which they see him and his flock;

and they see the barren mountains
they have been upon
and come off from.

And therefore

all you that be gathered into the name of Jesus,
and walk in the path of the just,
where the footsteps of the flock are,
quench not the spirit in any,

and if any will not have
of your bread of life, and water of life,
let them fast, that will neither
receive, nor give;

for the bread of life and water of life,
are not only given to feed yourselves,
but by them you may feed others,
and refresh others:

therefore

have bread in your houses,
and water in your own well,
and fruit of your own tree,
and salt in yourselves, to savour withal,
that you may try all things;

and have oil in your own lamps,
that they may burn in your own temple;
and odour and frankincense,
that it may burn continually upon your own altar. . . .

For the light that shines in your hearts
will give you the knowledge of the glory of God
in the face of Jesus Christ,

that you may know the heavenly treasure
in your earthly vessels,
and the day star to arise,
the day to dawn in your own hearts,

that you may become temples of Christ;
he to dwell with you,
and walk with you,
and sup with you;

and the blood of Christ
to sprinkle your hearts from dead works,
and your consciences also,
that you may serve the living God. . . .

And know the true word in your hearts and mouths;
which is the word of faith the apostle preached. . . .
Which is as a hammer to hammer down sin and evil,
and as a sword to cut it down,
and as a fire to burn it up. . . .

So all be diligent in the truth,
that you may be fruitful in the word of God,
that it may have its passage through you all.

The Bright Morning Star (Epistle 280, 1670)

Introductory Note

This beautiful epistle is a word of comfort "in the stormy time of night." This epistle offers several images for contemplation: What does it mean to you to have a "habitation" in God? What does your spiritual habitation look like? Can you see the "bright morning star" expelling darkness from your hearts?

Scripture

I Jesus have sent mine angel to testify unto you these things in the churches. I am the root and the offspring of David, *and* the bright and morning star.
Revelation 22:16 (KJV)

Through the tender mercy of our God;
whereby the dayspring from on high hath visited us
To give light to them that sit in darkness
and *in* the shadow of death,
to guide our feet into the way of peace.
Luke 1:78–79 (KJV)

Epistle

All dear Friends every where, . . .

let your cries and prayers be to him,
from whom all your help and strength comes;
who with his eternal power,
hath kept up your heads above
all waves and storms.

Let none go out of their habitations
in the stormy time of the night,
whose habitation is in the Lord;

let every one keep his habitation,
and stand in his lot,
the seed, Christ Jesus,
to the end of the day. . . .

[I]n this seed you will see
the bright and morning star appear,
which will expel the night of darkness
that hath been in your hearts;

by which morning star you will come
to the everlasting day,
which was before night was.

So every one feel this bright morning star
in your hearts,
there to expel the darkness.

The Suffering that Overcomes (Epistle 346, 1677)

Introductory Note

Fox asks Friends to persist in the way of nonviolent love despite the suffering they are enduring. Addressed *To Friends at Sussex*, Fox weaves together Isaiah's description of the Suffering Servant and Paul's hymn to love to encourage Friends to believe that suffering infused with love has the strength "to wear out all evil doers."

Scripture

I gave my back to the smiters, and my cheeks to them that plucked
off the hair: I hid not my face from shame and spitting.
Isaiah 50:6 (KJV)

He was oppressed, and he was afflicted, yet he opened not his
mouth: he is brought as a lamb to the slaughter, and as a sheep
before her shearers is dumb, so he openeth not his mouth.
Isaiah 53:7 (KJV)

Love suffreth long: it is bountifull: love envieth not:
love doeth not boast it selfe: it is not puffed up:
It doeth no uncomely thing: it seeketh not her own things:
it is not provoked to anger: it thinketh not evill:
It rejoyceth not in iniquitie, but rejoyceth in the trueth:

It suffreth all things: it beleeveth all things:
it hopeth all things: it endureth all things
1 Corinthians 13:4–7 (GNV)

Epistle

My dear friends,—

To whom is my love, and to the rest of Friends that aways. And my desire is, that you may all suffer as lambs of Christ;

for "when he was reviled, he reviled not again";
and he gave his back and cheek to the strikers and smiters,
and his hair to be plucked off,
and was as a "lamb led dumb before his shearers,
and he opened not his mouth";

though he was the King of kings, and Lord of lords:
and so left his followers and believers an example,
that they should follow him, like innocent lambs;

for the Lamb and the saints have the victory
over all the tearers, and strikers,
and pluckers, and devourers, and persecutors.

And so let patience have its perfect work in you and among you, in which you run the race, and do obtain the crown of eternal life.

And do not strive,
but keep down that spirit
that would strive,

with love,

which differeth you
from all other sufferers
that have not love,

which envieth not,
neither is provoked,
but beareth all things,
and endureth all things,
and will wear out all evil doers.

Prisoners, Show the Nature of the Lamb (Epistle 398, 1684)

Introductory Note

Here is a practical application of Jesus' teaching about loving our enemies. This is an excerpt from a long epistle Fox wrote from *London, the 3 d day of the 10 th month, 1684*, titled, *An epistle to all the prisoners and sufferers for the name of the Lord Jesus Christ and his worship*.

When difficulties arise it may be helpful to meditate on being "under the wings of Christ."

Note: Fox mentions dungeons and Bridewells. Bridewell was originally the name of a prison and orphanage in London; "Bridewell" came to be used in the names of many prisons and became a generic term for prison.

Scripture

But I say unto you, Love your enemies, bless them that curse you, do good to them that hate you, and pray for them which despitefully use you, and persecute you; That ye may be the children of your Father which is in heaven.
Matthew 5:44–45 (KJV)

He shall cover thee with his feathers, and under his wings shalt thou trust: his truth *shall be thy* shield and buckler.
Psalm 91:4 (KJV)

And when they bring you unto the synagogues, and *unto* magistrates, and powers, take ye no thought how or what thing ye shall answer, or what ye shall say: For the Holy Ghost shall teach you in the same hour what ye ought to say.
Luke 12:11–12 (KJV)

Epistle

Dear friends,

in the seed of life that is over all, . . .
it is not only given you to believe in the name of Christ,
but also to suffer for his name's sake. . . .

Now, dear friends and brethren,

if it doth please the Lord to try you,
who are the believers in the light,
and children of the light
and the day of Christ:

I say again,

if it please the Lord, and it be his will, to try you
in stinking prisons and dungeons,
Bridewells, houses of correction,
and suffer you to be put in such places,
who are his sheep and lambs,
plants and branches;

I say, the Lord can sanctify all such places

for his people,
his children,
his sons and daughters,
and make all pleasant to them:

for his sheep and people
cannot go any where from the Lord,
for the Lord and his presence is with them,
and the angel of his presence saves them;

and therefore

such jails and dungeons,
Bridewells, houses of correction,
which are for evil doers,

if the Lord do try, or suffer his people
to be put in such places,
yet his people are all in the hand,
and under the wings of Christ,

and he can sanctify
all such places to them.

And you, in that state,
are to pray for the enemies
that put you there;

and if they curse and hate you,
you are to bless them,
and to do good unto them,

and you are to pray for them
that despitefully use you,
and persecute you,

and love your enemies,
that you may be children
of your Father which is in heaven;

"for he maketh the sun to shine
on the evil and on the good,
and causeth his rain to fall
on the just and on the unjust" . . .

Now, dear friends and brethren, my desire is . . . that none are to question or take thought what they are to say; for it shall be given you in that same hour what ye shall speak, saith Christ; what any one of you doth want, God is all-sufficient to supply you; trust in him, and in fear walk before him. . . .

Love Overcomes (Epistle 417, 1689)

Introductory Note

One of Fox's last letters, he wrote this from *London, the 27 th of the 3 d month, 1689*, just months before the Toleration Act was assented to, ending the criminalization of Friends meetings.

Scripture

Beloved, let us love one another: for love is of God; and every one that loveth is born of God, and knoweth God. He that loveth not knoweth not God; for God is love.
1 John 4:7–8 (KJV)

Epistle

Dear friends and brethren in Christ Jesus, whom the Lord by his eternal arm and power hath preserved to this day, all walk in the power and spirit of God, that is over all, in love and unity.

For love overcomes,
and builds up and unites
all the members of Christ
to him, the head;
for love keeps out of all strife,
and is of God;

and love and charity never fail,
but keep the mind above all outward things,
or strife about outward things;
and is that which overcomes evil,
and casts out all false fears;

and it is of God,
and unites all the hearts of his people
together in the heavenly joy,
concord, and unity.

And the God of love
preserve you all,
and settle and establish you in Christ Jesus
your life and salvation,
in whom you have all peace with God.

And so, walk in him,
that you may be ordered
in his peaceable heavenly wisdom
to the glory of God,
and the comfort
one of another.

Amen.

Part Two: Gospel Order

And then I was moved of the Lord God to set up, and establish five Monthly Meetings of men and women in the city of London, besides the Women's Meeting and the Quarterly Meetings, to admonish, and exhort such as walked disorderly or carelessly, and not according to Truth; and to take care of God's glory.

And the Lord opened to me and let me see what I must do, and how I must order and establish the Men's and Women's Monthly and Quarterly Meetings in all the nation, and write to other nations, where I came not, to do the same.

George Fox *Journal*, for 1667 (Ni:511)

[A]ll men and women must lift up their eyes,
hands, hearts, and spirits to the Lord,
and to bow to him, and worship him;
and ought in all their meetings,
that gather in the name of Jesus,
to wait upon the Lord
for wisdom, counsel, and understanding, . . .
both in your men's and women's meetings,
and all other meetings
in the name of Jesus Christ,
for he is in the midst of them,
their prophet, priest, teacher,
shepherd, bishop, and counsellor. . . .
Epistle 313 (1674)

Introduction to Gospel Order

The epistles in Part One focused on the spiritual message of George Fox. They were mostly written in the 1650s and early 1660s during the period of the explosive growth of the Friends' movement. In Part Two, Fox advises Friends how to organize themselves around the revolutionary idea that it is possible for a society to come under the direct rule of Christ. In the 1660s and 1670s, Fox focused his work increasingly on establishing men's and women's meetings for that purpose.

Our Inward Teacher is also our Bishop. No human hierarchy may be allowed to usurp Christ's place. Business conducted with the intent of listening for the living Voice of God within each of us and drawing us into unity still has power to answer that of God in men and women and draw them into the eternal fellowship.

The Reign of Christ

Of the increase of *his* government and peace *there shall be* no end,
upon the throne of David, and upon his kingdom,
to order it, and to establish it
with judgment and with justice
from henceforth even for ever.
The zeal of the Lord of hosts will perform this.
Isaiah 9:7 (KJV)

Grafted into the Tree of Life (Epistle 354, 1679)

Introductory Note

Because it ties together Fox's understanding of how we are spiritually united with Christ and Fox's understanding of the church, this epistle serves as a good introduction to Gospel Order. Here we follow Fox's remarkable train of thought: Christ is the true head of the church. In the time of the established national churches, each so-called church had its own human head but none had the true head, Christ. Fox calls them "bodies without heads." They are monsters; we might say, zombies. Christ must be restored as the rightful head. How is this done?

Fox proceeds to a compelling and organic metaphor for the atonement: those who are "quickened [i.e., enlivened] by him [Christ], / and do believe in the light" are "grafted" into the tree of life, who is Christ. It is by being grafted into Christ and thus sharing Christ's holiness that we become "a spiritual household of faith." Here, Fox shifts the metaphor from branches grafted into the tree of life to the "living stones" of the true church.

It is the inclusive, holy, and counter-cultural life of the church which "answers that of God in all." Fox concludes with a call to "keep up the men and women's meetings." These are not conceived of as administrative bodies but are the vehicles in which Christ reigns in "an everlasting perfect fellowship and order." It was to this fellowship that Fox devoted the second part of his public ministry.

The epistle was written at *Swarthmore in Lancashire, the 30 th of the 11 th month, 1678*.

Scripture

And he shewed me a pure river of water of life, clear as crystal, proceeding out of the throne of God and of the Lamb. In the midst of the street of it, and on either side of the river, *was there* the tree of life, . . . and the leaves of the tree *were* for the healing of the nations. And there shall be no more curse: but the throne of God and of the Lamb shall be in it; and his servants shall serve him. . . . And there shall be no night there; and they need no candle, neither light of the sun; for the Lord God giveth them light: and they shall reign for ever and ever.
Revelation 22:1–3,5 (KJV)

I am the vine, ye *are* the branches: He that abideth in me, and I in him, the same bringeth forth much fruit: for without me ye can do nothing.
John 15:5 (KJV)

For both he that sanctifieth and they who are sanctified *are* all of one: for which cause he is not ashamed to call them brethren, Saying, I will declare thy name unto my brethren, in the midst of the church will I sing praise unto thee.
Hebrews 2:11–12 (KJV)

Epistle

And, dear friends, my love to you all

in the seed of life and peace,
which floweth as a river,
and bruiseth the head of the serpent. . . .

and in this seed Christ
is (sic) all nations blessed and elected;

and out of it is the curse. . . .
And out of this seed are
    all the false religions,
    false ways, false worships,
    and false churches, or

bodies without heads,
like so many monsters. . . .

Now this monstrous body is brought in by . . . such as are gone from the light, grace, truth, power, and spirit, that cometh from Christ, the heavenly head. . . . And, therefore, all must. . . . hold him their head, Christ, . . . who is first and last, the beginning and ending. Hallelujah. . . .

So with my love in the Lord,
    the Creator of all,
and in the Lord Jesus Christ,
    by whom was all,
    who is over all,
the first and last,

a living rock and foundation
for all the living to build upon,
that are quickened by him,
and do believe in his light,
which is the life in Christ,
the word, by whom all things were made;

and so are grafted into Christ,
the living tree, that never withereth;
and so from him the green tree
every graft doth receive its nourishment,
that is grafted into him;

and so the living root
doth bear every living branch, and nourishes it,

that it may bring forth fruit
to the praise of God over all, blessed for ever.

And this is the tree
whose leaf never fadeth,
nor fruit faileth;

but its fruit feedeth all the living,
and the leaves thereof
heal the nations.

And this tree stands in the midst of God's garden,
who saith, in the midst of thy church will I sing praise,
which are living stones, a spiritual household of faith,

elect and precious,
the church of the living God,
written in heaven;

so holiness becomes
the house of the Lord.

And therefore the Lord doth require more from Friends than all other people, because he hath given more to them; and so all people do expect more from Friends than all other people, in answering that of God in them all in truth and in righteousness, and holiness and godliness; for ye are the lights of the world, and the salt of the earth to season it. . . .

And therefore my desires are, that you may all be valiant for the truth upon the earth; and keep up all your men['s] and women's meetings in the Lord's power, the gospel, (which hath brought life and immortality to light) . . . in which gospel is an everlasting perfect fellowship and order, which will stand when all others are gone;

all the saints that do enjoy this,
  cannot but praise the Lord,
    and sing praises to him
      for ever and ever.

Amen.

Gospel Order: The Example of My Life (Epistle 308, 1674)

Introductory Note

Fox recalls, "when I turned you to him that is able to save you, I left you to him." This reflects Fox's extraordinary faith in the real presence of Christ, our Teacher, and in our ability to hear his teaching and obey it. This is the foundation for gospel order that is not based in a human hierarchy (with him at the top!). This is why we are known as Friends and not "Foxites." *Given forth in the time of his sickness in Worcester prison, 1674.*

Scripture

> And I saw another angel fly in the midst of heaven, having the everlasting gospel to preach unto them that dwell on the earth, and to every nation, and kindred, and tongue, and people.
>
> Revelation 14:6 (KJV)

Epistle

My dear friends in England, and all parts of the world; the gospel, which is the power of God, which you have received from the beginning, keep in it, and the fellowship of it; in which there is neither sect nor schism, but an everlasting fellowship, and an everlasting order. . . .

And therefore now the gospel order is to be set up again, and the government of Christ Jesus, by them that be heirs of him, and of his government. . . . For the foundation is already laid, which is Christ, and his government is set up. . . . And therefore, friends, if you keep under Christ, the governor, who governs his church in righteousness, and who is a prophet, and preacher, and keep in his gospel order; none . . . can deceive you, let them come with never so fair pretenses. . . .

[It Is Christ Alone Who Is Lord.]

And therefore it concerns all that profess themselves to be ministers, to be humble, else they are no learners of Christ; not to be harsh nor high minded, but walk as examples amongst God's flock, and not to be lords over God's inheritance; but let him be Lord whose right it is, &c.

And you have known the manner of my life, the best part of thirty years, since I went forth, and forsook all things;

I sought not myself,
I sought you
and his glory that sent me;

and when I turned you to him
that is able to save you,
I left you to him:

and my travels have been great,
in hungers and colds,
when there were few,
for the first six or seven years . . .

I often lay in woods
and commons in the night;
that many times it was
as a by-word, that I would not
come into houses, and lie in their beds.

And the prisons have been made my home
a great part of my time,
and in danger of my life,
and in jeopardy daily.

And amongst you
I have made myself of no reputation,
to keep the truth up in reputation. . . .

With the low, I made myself low;
and with the weak and feeble,
I was as one with them,

and condescended to all conditions,
for the Lord had fitted me so
before he sent me forth;

and so I passed through
great sufferings in my body,
as you have been sensible.

[Men and Women: Possessors of the Heavenly Gospel Order.]

And few at the first took care for the establishing men['s] and women's meetings, though they were generally owned when they understood them: but the everlasting God, that sent me forth by his everlasting power, first to declare his everlasting gospel, and then after people had received the gospel, I was moved to go through the nation, to advise them to set up the men's meetings, and the women's, many of which were set up; and I was moved to write to other places, for them to do the like, that kept the power.

And this was the end,
that all that had received the gospel,
might be possessors of it,
and of the gospel order,
    which is heavenly;

and that all that had received Christ Jesus,
might so walk in him,
and possess his government
in the church, who are members of him
    the heavenly head.

And so men and women
being heirs of Christ,
they are heirs of him,
and of his government: . . .

which is an everlasting order,
which is from the power of God;

for the gospel is called,
the everlasting gospel.

So that all now in the restoration
by Christ Jesus, into the image of God,
may be helps-meet in holiness and righteousness,
as Adam and Eve were in before they fell;

for in the church of Christ,
where he is head,
 there is his gospel,
 and his order,
 and his government;

there is his power felt
in every one's heart,

and there are these offices
 of admonishing, rebuking,
 exhorting, reproving,
 amongst them that are convinced. . . .

Know Christ in All His Offices (Epistle 304, 1673)

Introductory Note

It is by knowing Christ "in all his offices" (prophet, teacher, priest, bishop, etc.) that followers of Christ are able to reject a human hierarchy of priests and clergy, bishops and popes. When we have Christ within us and—crucially—"among us" as a community of believers, we have the substance of which those human religious authorities are only figures. In and through his offices, Christ expresses his headship in the church. Fox insists that this is true, not in some ethereal or spiritual way only but in the practical business and pastoral life of the church.

The epistle was initially addressed to *Friends in Virginia*. from *Worcester, 1673,* with the instruction *Read this amongst Friends in their meetings*. At the time of writing, Fox explains, he was in prison, ironically having been "premunired" for refusing to take an oath denying the Pope's supremacy, pleading that Jesus himself had forbidden all oaths. The penalty was forfeiture of property, civil rights, and imprisonment at the King's pleasure (OED; Jones:484–485).

Scripture

And he shall send Jesus Christ, . . . For Moses truly said unto the fathers, A prophet shall the Lord your God raise up unto you.
Acts 3:20, 22 (KJV)

For ye were as sheep going astray; but are now returned unto the Shepherd and Bishop of your souls.
1 Peter 2:25 (KJV)

But Christ being come an high priest . . . who through the eternal Spirit offered himself without spot to God.
Hebrews 9:11, 14 (KJV)

That he might sanctify and cleanse it with the washing of water by the word, That he might present it to himself a glorious church, not having spot, or wrinkle, or any such thing; but that it should be holy and without blemish.
Ephesians 5:26–27 (KJV)

Epistle

Dear friends, to whom is my love, I am glad to hear of the increase of truth amongst you, and the Lord prosper his work. . . . [T]here is no salvation by any other name under heaven, but by the name of Jesus. . . .

And in his name
keep your men's and women's,
and all your other meetings,
that you may feel him in the midst of you,
exercising his offices;

as he is a prophet,
which God has raised up
to open to you,

and as he is a shepherd,
who has laid down his life for you,
to feed you, so hear his voice;

and as he is a counselor,
and a commander,
follow him and his counsel;

and as he is a bishop
to oversee you,
with his heavenly power and spirit;

and as he is a priest,
who offered up himself for you,
who is made higher than the heavens, . . .
who sanctifies his people, his church,
and presents them to God
without blemish, spot, or wrinkle:

so, I say,
know him in all his offices,
exercising them amongst you,
and in you. . . .

I have been a prisoner here about these eight months, and now I am premunired, because I cannot take an oath; but the Lord's seed and power is over all, blessed be his name for ever . . .

Conduct of Meetings in Gospel Order (Epistle 313, 1674)

Introductory Note

In these excerpts from a longer epistle, Fox emphasizes the importance of waiting to feel the presence of Jesus in the midst of those who seek to conduct meetings for church business. The unity of the body is a sign of Christ's government; disunity is a sign of too little "stillness and quietness in the pure spirit of God."

Scripture

> I therefore, the prisoner of the Lord, beseech you that ye walk worthy of the vocation wherewith ye are called, With all lowliness and meekness, with longsuffering, forbearing one another in love; Endeavouring to keep the unity of the Spirit in the bond of peace.
>
> Ephesians 4:1–3 (KJV)

Epistle

[A]ll men and women must lift up their eyes,
hands, hearts, and spirits to the Lord,
and to bow to him, and worship him;

and ought in all their meetings,
that gather in the name of Jesus,
to wait upon the Lord
for wisdom, counsel, and understanding,

that by it they may be ordered and directed
in his holy service and business,
in his holy church,
which Christ is the holy head of,

as they are directed and ordered
by the Lord's power and wisdom,
to praise, and magnify, and glorify him,
          with thanksgiving,

both in your men's and women's meetings,
and all other meetings
in the name of Jesus Christ,

for he is in the midst of them,
their prophet, priest, teacher,
shepherd, bishop, and counsellor,

opening with his heavenly power,
feeding with his heavenly food,
counselling with his heavenly counsel,

          sanctifying them,

to present them to the holy God without spot,
overseeing them with his holy power and spirit;
that God may have the praise and the glory

          through Jesus Christ,
          in all, and through all,
          who is blessed for ever.

So Friends are not to meet
like a company of people
about town or parish business,

neither in their men's
nor women's meetings,
but to wait upon the Lord;

and feeling his power
and spirit to lead them,
and order them to his glory;

that so whatsoever they may do,
they may do it to the praise and glory of God,
and in unity in the faith, and in the spirit,
and in fellowship in the order of the gospel. . . .

[T]here has so much strife and foolishness entered into the minds of people, and a want of the stillness and quietness in the pure spirit of God. . . . But wait all in the diligence, in the holy life, by which the holy things are seen and received, in which the holy unity and fellowship is. So no more but my love.

False "Growth in Truth" (Epistle 228, 1663)

Introductory Note

This letter, inscribed *Lancaster prison the 6 th day* concerns the question of how to discern a true movement of the Holy Spirit from something false or "notional." It seems likely that the "something . . . not right" that Fox says he feels amongst Friends concerns John Perrot, a Friend whose emphasis on the authority of the Light within the individual ran up against the unity of the fellowship. Should Friends meet for worship at regularly stated times and places, or should Friends meet only as led by the Spirit? Should all the men remove their hats as a testimony to God's sovereignty when someone is offering vocal prayer (Fox's position), or should each Friend discern whether to remove their hat for himself (Perrot's position)? In his *Journal* for 1664 (Ni:474), Fox says he issued a warning to Friends against "that spirit that wrought in John Perrot and his company against the Truth."

In a fellowship that exalts each individual's ability to hear and obey Christ, the Inward Teacher, where can we find unity in our faith and practice? Fox sees a ground for discernment in the spiritual fruit: high-mindedness and strife are signs that something is not right.

Scripture

And why beholdest thou the mote that is in thy brother's eye, but considerest not the beam that is in thine own eye? Or how wilt thou say to thy brother, Let me pull out the mote out of thine eye; and, behold, a beam *is* in thine own eye? Thou hypocrite, first cast out the beam out of thine own eye; and then shalt thou see clearly to cast out the mote out of thy brother's eye.

Matthew 7:3–5 (KJV)

Epistle

Dear friends, who have tasted of that which is precious, and have felt the truth convincing of you; and also felt the power of the Lord God:

I feel something
amongst some of you
that is not right;

and how that such get up
into the wise part,
but are out of the power,
and out of the life,

and with that judge,
and are beholding the moats in others eyes,
whilst the beam is in their own eyes.

Oh! abuse not the power,
in which is the gospel fellowship,
which will keep all in unity,

and grieve not the spirit,
in which is the true fellowship,
and the bond of peace.

Keep down high-mindedness,
despise not prophecies,

and quench not the spirit in the least,
for that is flesh and not spirit in yourselves
            that doth so.

Judge not before the time
that the Lord do come,
who brings to light all the hidden things
of darkness in you;

run not into outward things,
that is the fleshly mind,
that will run from one thing,
and so be restless,
and will not know what seat to sit in;

after it hath been in one outward thing
it will run into another,
and call it, his growth in the truth,
and fall a judging others;
but that judgment is after the flesh,
and their growth is in the flesh;

the fruits of it
is strife, backbitings, whisperings,
and leads to idleness,
            busy-bodies from house to house,
            slandering, scandalizing, vilifying,
and are in lightness,
out of the fear of God,
in variance and sowing dissention. . . .

So the fruits of every birth manifesteth itself;

the fruits of the spirit are
love, and peace,
and truth, and plainness,
and righteousness, and godliness.

> But the fruits of the flesh are
> backbitings, whisperings,
> lyings, slanderings, scandalizings. . . .

And therefore mind your first habitation and first love, and that which did convince you, that you may all come into life and power, to sit down in the habitation of it, in love, and life, and unity. . . .

Against Reasonings and Disputes (Epistle 244, 1666)

Introductory Note

The ultimate goal is for Christ to rule in all things. Whatever challenges this rule must be swept away like rubbish. Here is a radical call for Friends to rely on "the power of God" rather than on "carnal reason." We can too easily rely on planning exercises and human calculation or compromise when we really need to be waiting in silent yieldedness for the Spirit. The question arises, do we really want to be spiritually "naked to God, and to one another"? Fox addressed this epistle *To Friends in Barbadoes, Virginia, Maryland, New England, and elsewhere*.

Note "besom," a word found in Isaiah, simply means "broom."

Scripture

> I will sweep it [Babylon] with the besom of
> destruction, saith the LORD of hosts.
> Isaiah 14:23 (KJV)

Epistle

O friends!—

You all that have tasted of the power of the Lord God, and of his truth, . . . whatsoever is gotten up through the carnal reason, . . . let that be purged out of your hearts; if not, it will lift up your hearts to consultations, subtilty, questionings, reasonings, and disputes. Oh! I feel too much of that which hath gotten up into the wrong understanding part . . . and the power of God hath not the supremacy in all your hearts. . . .

Oh! cleanse, cleanse, cleanse,
and join to the pure immortal power;
for the power of the Lord God
will make room for itself. . . .

The besom of the Lord is going forth to sweep,
the candle of the Lord is lighted
to search every corner of your houses;
for the just walk in the path
which is a shining light,
which admits of no rubbish in it. . . .

Therefore keep out strife,
keep out fornication and the adulterous spirit;
keep out the lusts of the eye,
the lusts of the flesh,
        and pride of life . . .

that all your eyes, minds, and hearts
may be kept single and naked
        to God, and to one another;
and unclothed of all that which is contrary,
        and is got up since.

For the seed, the life of Christ Jesus,
        reigns and rules:
        glory to him for ever. . . .

TESTIMONIES

And they overcame him by the blood of the Lamb,
and by the word of their testimony;
and they loved not their lives unto the death.
Revelation 12:11 (KJV)

Keep Your Testimonies (Epistle 263, 1668)

Introductory Note

Originally titled, *An exhortation to keep to the ancient principles of truth*, this epistle presents two lists of testimonies that are very different than most contemporary lists of Quaker testimonies. Even though specific practices may change over time, enduring values may be at stake. Some parts of Fox's advice sound strikingly contemporary: make restitution to those who have been wronged; do true judgment, justice, and equity.

The first two items, "keep at a word" and "keep to the sound language," refer to two aspects of plain speech. The first refers to naming a single fair price rather than bargaining; the second has to do with refusing to use the honorific plural "you" when addressing a single person of rank.

In between the two lists is a section, which begins, "And Friends, live all in the power of God." Here, Fox brings up the knotty and intertwined issues of authority to make judgment, the importance of mercy, and the danger of what he calls "foolish pity." Notably, he warns against giving special favor to family, beloved acquaintances, or showing "any respect of persons," which means the upper class or wealthy. The epistle closes with a short section on how to deal with disagreements among us, a topic more fully addressed in Epistle 264 (b).

Scripture

But the wisdom that is from above is first pure, then peaceable, gentle, and easy to be intreated, full of mercy and good fruits, without partiality, and without hypocrisy.
James 3:17 (KJV)

Epistle

Friends,

keep at a word in all your dealings without oppression.

And keep to the sound language, thou to every one.

And keep your testimony against the world's vain fashions.

And keep your testimony against the hireling priests, and their tithes, and maintenance. . . .

And against the priests' and the world's joining in marriages.

And your testimony against swearing, and the world's corrupt manners.

And against all looseness, pleasures, and profaneness whatsoever.

And against all the world's evil ways, vain worships, and religions, and to stand up for God's.

And to see that restitution be made by every one, that hath done wrong to any. . . .

And, friends, live all in the power of the Lord God, . . . and in the light, life, truth, and power of God do true judgment, justice, and truth, righteousness, and equity in all your men['s] and women's meetings, without favour or affection to relations, kindreds, and acquaintance, or any respect of persons. . . .

Let mercy overshadow the judgment seat, and let mercy be mixed with judgment.

Take heed of foolish pity; and if you be not diligent against all profaneness, sin, iniquity, and uncleanness, looseness, and debauchery, and that which dishonoureth God, then you let those things come up upon you, which you should be atop of. . . . And in all your men['s] and women's meetings, let all things be done in love, which doth edify the body; and . . . in the wisdom of God, which is pure and gentle, from above. . . .

> And keep your testimony for your liberty in Christ Jesus, and stand fast in it, against all . . . the false and loose liberties in the flesh.
>
> And train up all your children in the fear of the Lord, and in his new covenant, Christ Jesus. . . .
>
> And let no man or any live to themselves, but in that love that seeks not her own. . . .
>
> And that Friends do keep in their testimony against . . . idle tippling, and taking tobacco in coffee houses and alehouses, which is an ill savour.
>
> And against all strife and contention whatsoever.

And that some Friends be appointed at every meeting to keep the doors, to keep down rude boys and unruly spirits; that so the meetings may be kept civil and quiet.

And if one Friend hath any thing against another, let him not treasure it up, . . . but let him presently speak to the Friend. . . . that things may not be deferred too long . . . but that they may be answered in a short time, lest they be put to a strait in the matter. And stop all bad reports, (for thou shalt not raise a false report upon my people, saith the Lord,) and minister justice upon it presently, so that no man or woman may be defiled or defamed with such things.

Read this in the Men['s] and Women's Meetings in the fear of the Lord, as often as you see occasion, and record it in your book.

The Line of Righteousness and Justice (Epistle 200, 1661)

Introductory Note

In this epistle, Fox makes economic justice a core testimony. In our time of climate change-induced fire and flood, I am particularly struck by Fox's insistence that good work "doth not spoil, nor destroy, nor waste the creation on the lusts." Significant, as well, is Fox's opposition to debt, that snare to the unwary and engine of capitalist wealth creation, which Fox charges with being a "destroyer of creation."

These excerpts are drawn from a lengthy tract-like epistle with this expansive title: *The line of righteousness and justice stretched forth over all merchants, &c. And an exhortation unto all Friends and people whatsoever, who are merchants, tradesmen, husbandmen, or seamen, who deal in merchandise, trade in buying and selling by sea or land, or deal in husbandry, that ye all do that which is just, equal, and righteous in the sight of God and man, one to another, and to all men. And that ye use just weights and just measures, and speak and do that which is true, just, and right in all things. That so your conversations, lives, practices, and tongues may preach to all people, and answer the good, just, and righteous principle of God in them all. In which ye may be serviceable unto God, and to the creation in your generation, and a blessing both to God and man.*

Fox appended these verses from Proverbs at the close of the epistle:

Scripture

He that walketh in his integritie, is just:
and blessed shall his children be after him.
Proverbs 20:7 (GNV)

Divers weightes, and divers measures,
both these are even abomination unto the Lord.
Proverbs 20:10 (GNV)

Owe no man any thing, but to love one another: for
he that loveth another hath fulfilled the law.
Romans 13:8 (KJV)

Epistle

All Friends, every where, live in the seed of God, which is the righteousness itself. . . .

Do rightly, justly, truly, hol[ily], equally
to all people in all things;

and that is according to that of God in every man,
and the witness of God,
and the wisdom of God,
and the life of God in yourselves;

and there ye are serviceable in your generation,
labouring in the thing that is good,
which doth not spoil, nor destroy,
nor waste the creation upon the lusts.

And all merchants whatsoever, seamen, and traffickers by sea or land; this is the word of the Lord God to you all: "Do justly, speak truly, to all people whatsoever." . . . "Wrong no man, overreach no man," if it may be never so much to your advantage, but be plain, righteous, and holy. . . . Loathe deceit and all unrighteousness, hard-heartedness, wronging, cozening, cheating, or unjust dealing . . . and that will win people to deal with you. . . . And so here your lives and words will preach wherever ye come.

All husbandmen, and dealers about husbandry whatsoever, cattle, or ground, to you all this is the word of the Lord God: do rightly, holily, justly, honestly, plainly, and truly to all men and people, whomsoever ye have to deal withal; wrong not any in any case, though it be never so much to your advantage. Deny yourselves, and live in the cross of Christ, the power of God, for that destroys injustice. . . .

So all Friends, of what calling soever, that dwell in the power of God, and feel the power of God, and the light of Christ Jesus: dwell in that, act in that; that ye may answer that of God in every one upon the earth with your actions, and by your conversations, and by your words. . . .

And all, of what trade or calling soever,

keep out of debts;
owe to no man any thing but love.

Go not beyond your estates,
lest ye bring yourselves to trouble,
and cumber, and a snare;
keep low and down in all things ye act.

For a man that would be great,
and goes beyond his estate,
lifts himself up, runs into debt,
and lives highly of other men's means;
he is a waster of other men's,
and a destroyer. He is not serviceable to the creation,
but a destroyer of the creation and creatures,
and cumbereth himself and troubleth others. . . .

Owe to none any thing but love;
and in that ye will feel the blessing. . . .

For Friends, if ye be not faithful in the outward treasure, and outward mammon, who will trust you with the true treasure? . . . So, I say to you all, see that ye are faithful in this outward mammon, this outward treasure of the things of this life, of this world, faithful to your word, faithful to your days, faithful to your promises. . . .

For God will have a holy people,
to serve him in holiness;

a true people,
to serve him in truth,
and in his spirit,
and in his new and living way . . .

So the Lord God Almighty keep and preserve you
faithful in all things
to his glory and honour for ever!

Cry Out for Justice and Equity (Epistle 251, 1667)

Introductory Note

Although economic justice does not appear on most contemporary lists of Quaker testimonies, the practice of naming a fair price and refusing to bargain was an early testimony. Here, Fox recounts the history of suffering for the single price testimony, followed by its acceptance. (See more on this in Epistle 131.) In this, we also hear a hint of Fox's memory of early Quaker prophets crying out for justice and equity in the public sphere.

Note: Along with emphasis on economic justice, Fox speaks of equity. For Fox, business practices are not private matters separated from the life of faith but matters of faithfulness to the power of God and central to answering that of God in others.

Scripture

Wherefore also we pray always for you, that our God would count you worthy of *this* calling, and fulfil all the good pleasure of *his* goodness, and the work of faith with power:
2 Thessalonians 1:11 (KJV)

I press toward the mark for the prize of the
high calling of God in Christ Jesus.
Philippians 3:14 (KJV)

But let judgment run down as waters, and
righteousness as a mighty stream.
Amos 5:24 (KJV)

Epistle

My dear friends . . . now Friends are become a people gathered in the holy name of Jesus. Therefore all are to walk worthy of the high calling of God in Christ Jesus . . .; that in that your life may shine before men, to answer that of God in all.

And so, walk in the light
as children of the light
and of the day.

For you know that formerly
we did cry against the powers of the earth,
because that judgment,
and justice,
and righteousness
did not run down their streets.

And now that Friends
are become a great people,
shall not judgment,
and justice,
and righteousness
run down our streets as a stream and a flood,
to drive away all the filth from amongst us?

And now that Friends are become a good savour in the hearts of all people, . . . lose it not; . . . for at first ye know that many could not take so much money in your trade as to buy bread with; all people stood aloof of you, when you stood upright, and gave them the plain language, and were at a word; but now . . . they will trust you before their own people, knowing that you will not cheat, nor wrong, nor cozen, nor oppress them. For the cry is now . . . where is there a Quaker of such and such a trade? So that they will deal with Friends before they will deal with their own. Oh! therefore friends, who have purchased this through great sufferings, lose not this great favour which God hath given unto you, but that you may answer the witness of God in every man. . . .

And now, friends, if there be any oppression, exaction, or defrauding . . . the world will see such, and say, the Quakers are not as they were; therefore such should be exhorted to equity and truth.

And also, if any run into debt, and aim at great things, and make a great show in the world of other's goods, which comes to burden others, . . . and oppress them, . . . such must be exhorted to justice, equity, and righteousness, and an even measure, to do as they would be done by. . . .

> That justice, judgment, and righteousness may flow
> as a river, and as a stream,
> and drive away all the filth from among us;
>
> that nothing but the power of God,
> and the life of truth, may rule amongst us. . . .
> So that every one . . . mind
> the Lord's business above their own.
>
>   And every one
> be tender of the glory of God,
>   and be careful,
> that in nowise his name and truth
>   be dishonoured.

[PS] *So let this be read in all your men*['s] *and women's meetings, who are to take notice of all such things. So no more, but my love in the universal seed of God, which never sinned, which is first and last, the top and corner-stone.*

Nations Shall Not Learn War Any More (Epistle 188, 1659)

Introductory Note

The "peace testimony" is probably the most widely known distinctive of Friends, but in 1659, when this epistle was written, it was still being formulated. It was a "time great stirs were in the nation." According to his Journal, this prompted Fox to write an epistle: "All Friends, everywhere, keep out of plots and bustling. . . . All that pretend to fight for Christ are deceived, for his kingdom is not of this world, therefore his servants do not fight. . . . Live in peace, in Christ, the way of peace, and therein seek the peace of all men, and no man's hurt" (Ni:356–357).

In another such epistle, Fox here warns Friends against "blending yourselves with the outward powers." There is a legitimate power of government to put down law breakers, but ultimately, having killed with the sword, they "must perish by the sword." Instead, Friends are called to "take away the occasion of wars." Peace follows where "the reign of Christ is known."

Scripture

And he shall judge among the nations, and shall rebuke many people: and they shall beat their swords into plowshares, and their spears into pruninghooks: nation shall not lift up sword against nation, neither shall they learn war any more.
Isaiah 2:4 (KJV)

Then said Jesus unto him, Put up again thy sword into his place: for all they that take the sword shall perish with the sword.
Matthew 26:52 (KJV)

Epistle

Friends,—

Live in the seed of God that destroys the devil,
who is the author and cause of wars and strife,
and bringing of men and people into the earth,
where the war, strife, and pride are;

here the outward swordsmen
have not learned yet
to beat their swords and spears
into ploughshares and pruning hooks.

Yet ye that are in that seed, see that ye accuse no man falsely, that hath the sword of justice, which is to keep the peace, and is a terror to the evil doers, and to keep down the transgressors, and for the praise of them that do well; this is owned in its place. But he that killeth with the sword, must perish with the sword.

So there was a time . . . to fight with outward weapons, with sword, and spear; but there is a time, when nations shall not learn war any more, but shall come to that which shall take away the occasion of wars, which was in the beginning before wars were. And Friends take heed of blending yourselves with the outward powers of the earth.

All Friends,

dwell in the life, and power, and seed of God,
in which ye may be kept in the son of God's kingdom,
and preserved in his dominion
out of all changeable things;
in that God's blessing will be with you.

In the seed of God is the stayed state,
and in that are the life and peace with God. . . .
And there the reign of Christ is known,
who is come to reign and to rule.

Keep to the Single Language (Epistle 191, 1660)

Introductory Note

The "single language" was, for Fox, a testimony that "slays the world's honour." In seventeenth-century England, a person lower in the social hierarchy was required to honor a person of higher rank by using the plural form, "you," whereas the higher-ranked person used the singular "thee" to someone of lower rank. Friends insisted on "thee and thou" to people, regardless of rank. As culture changed, the Quaker "thee and thou" became an in-group form of endearment. It is worth considering what counter-cultural practices today "slays the world's honor."

Fox wanted this epistle to be widely read, adding, "*Let this be sent abroad, that all may read it over.*"

Scripture

> If ye fulfill the royal law according to the scripture, Thou shalt love thy neighbour as thyself, ye do well: But if ye have respect to persons, ye commit sin, and are convinced of the law as transgressors.
>
> James 2:8–9 (KJV)

Epistle

All Friends every where, that are convinced with truth, and profess it, and own it, keep to the single language . . . And so, do not lose that testimony, which slays the world's honour, and do not go into the custom of the world's fashions . . . for there must be, and always was a distinction betwixt one and many. . . . So let Friends be distinct from all the world in their language, in their ways, in love, and in their conversations; . . .

> distinguish singular from plural,
> many things from one thing,
> and one from two and three;

and many men and women from one,
many ways from one,
many churches from one,
many fellowships from one,

and the many words from one,
and the many gods from one,
and the true Christ
from the many antichrists and false.

All this is distinguished and known by the one spirit, the light and power of Christ Jesus, which gives an understanding.

You Are Called to Holiness and Chastity (Epistle 168, 1658)

Introductory Note

In Fox's day, there was an informal movement, the so-called "Ranters," who claimed that since Christ had taken away all sin, we are free to do as we please—eat, drink, have sex—all the while claiming to be "led of the spirit." Against this, Fox calls for holiness and chastity as a testimony that Christ's power enables us to live lives ordered by the wisdom of God. How might "holiness and chastity" be expressed in our day?

Fox uses the phrase, "fond affections, and fond love" meaning "foolishly tender." He is probably warning against going too far in a relationship we might call a "crush."

Scripture

Know ye not that the unrighteous shall not inherit the kingdom of God? Be not deceived: neither fornicators, nor idolaters, nor adulterers.

1 Corinthians 6:9 (KJV)

For all that is in the world, the lust of the flesh, and the lust of the eyes, and the pride of life, is not of the Father, but is of the world.
1 John 2:16 (KJV)

Epistle

Friends all every where, who have tasted of the love, mercy, and kindness of God, and his power, ye are called to holiness and chastity.

Therefore,

keep out of inordinate affections,
and inordinate fleshly love,
and feigned flattery and desires,
which are below the truth;
which will bring you to infirmness.

And keep out of fond affections, and fond love,
that draws out the fleshly part, the fleshly eye,
and brings into pride, and looseness, and false liberty,
and to abuse the power of God.

Oh! keep out of all uncleanness,
whatever may be pretended,
and fleshly desires;

for the "lust of the eye,
the lust of the flesh,
and the pride of life
are not of the Father, but of the world."

And therefore. keep down that which is not of the Father, but of the world. And take heed of dishonouring your bodies, and defiling your minds . . . but live pure, chaste, and holy, as becometh the saints; for no adulterer nor fornicator hath any part in the kingdom of God. Such go from that of God in themselves, and quench the spirit of God, and abuse his power, and go into fleshly love, and feigned desires, and flattering pretences, covering it with a false liberty, and so are in the bondage to the beggarly, fleshly lusts; and whom they overcome, they bring into the same bondage. . . .

Therefore live in the truth, for all . . . that go into uncleanness under what fair pretence soever, are to be judged.

Regarding Marriage (Epistle 264(a), 1669)

Introductory Note

This is the first of four extracts from the lengthy Epistle 264. It was actually a collection of material gathered from other epistles as is made clear in its original title, *An additional extract from other of G. F.'s Epistles, both of former and latter dates, more largely speaking to things contained in the paper foregoing, with some new matters; recommended to Friends by him, (from time to time,) to be taken notice of at their Quarterly and other meetings*.

The same year of this epistle, Margaret Fell and George Fox exchanged marriage vows with each other in a large gathering of Friends held in Bristol, England. They seem to have followed the practices laid out in this epistle. They first cleared the proposed wedding with the children of Margaret Fell and Judge Fell (who had died eleven years earlier) to insure that the marriage would not deprive the children of inheritances still owed them from their father. The couple then presented their proposed marriage "before several meetings, both of the men and women, . . . and all were satisfied. . . . Then was a certificate, relating both the proceeding and the marriage, openly read and signed" by relations and Friends (Ni:554–555).

Over the years, the procedure for marriage under the care of Friends has remained much as laid out here. The radical equality of the couple who marry each other before God and witnessed by Friends continues as a vital testimony. With discontinuance of separate men's and women's business meetings, we have necessarily made adjustments. Note that, for those times when Friends found a reason for the wedding not to proceed, Fox gives Friends ample room for quietly ending the process before the matter becomes public.

Note: Fox opens with a passionate exhortation not to be married by "priests" whose "hands are dipped in the blood of our brethren in New England." This refers to the execution by hanging in Boston of Friends William Robinson and Marmaduke Stevenson, on 27th October, 1659; Mary Dyer, on 1st June, 1660; and William Leddra, on 14th March, 1661 (Ni:411, fn 2).

Note also: In these excerpts, Fox repeatedly speaks of marriage as between "male and female." In recent decades, many Friends Meetings (including my own) have felt led to say that gender does not matter for right marriage. This raises the question, what is "eternal" among Friends concerning sexual relations, and what is merely cultural, and how do we discern the difference?

Scripture

> And he answered and said unto them, Have ye not read, that he which made them at the beginning made them male and female, And said, For this cause shall a man leave father and mother, and shall cleave to his wife: and they twain shall be one flesh? Wherefore they are no more twain, but one flesh. What therefore God hath joined together, let not man put asunder.
>
> Matthew 19:4–6 (KJV)

Epistle

[Regarding Those Who Marry before a Priest]

And all such as marry by the priests, who have . . . had their hands dipped in the blood of our brethren in New England, and who have . . . spoiled so many of their goods, casting them into prisons . . .: must come to judgment and condemnation of themselves, or else Friends . . . must write and bear their testimony against them both . . . let them be three or four times admonished, that they may have gospel order, so that if it be possible, they may come to that which at first did convince them, and to repent. . . .

[Marriage is God's Work]

For it is not the bishops' nor priests' work to marry people; . . . nor you never read throughout the holy scriptures, that either priests or bishops married any; but it is God's work, and his ordinance; for whom God joins together, let no man put asunder.

And marriage is honourable in all, the bed being undefiled. And they took one another in the assemblies of the righteous, the saints, and the holy ones of God, who were of the seed of the righteous. Which practice is now followed amongst the people of God, called Quakers, who are of the seed and generation of the righteous, the elect people of God.

And so marriage was a figure of Christ and his church, as the apostle instanceth in Ephesians. And therefore they were not to be unequally yoked, believers with unbelievers. . . . And such . . . go contrary to the law of God, and grieve him and their righteous parents. . . .

So marriage is God's holy ordinance, and Christ, that comes to restore all things again into their place, saith, "Whom God joins together, let no man put asunder." And brings it to the beginning again, how God made them male and female.

So in the restoration in the image of God and sanctification, they are brought to the joining one male with one female again; not for one man to have many women at once, God did not make many for him; but in the fall from the righteousness of God and his image, there they run together like beasts, a man and many women. There men join and put asunder; "but in the beginning it was not so," saith Christ, the heavenly man, the second Adam, "for God made them male and female, and whom he joins together, let no man put asunder."

And so God joins with his spirit and power, for he is a spirit; and this is a heavenly and spiritual joining; and them that God joins, they do not follow strange flesh, but the spirit of God; and such a marriage is sanctified by the spirit, and by the Lord, and such know his heavenly ordinance. . . .

For the right joining in marriage is the work of the Lord only, and not the priests or magistrates; for it is God's ordinance, and not man's. And therefore Friends cannot consent, that they should join them together. For we marry none, it is the Lord's work, and we are but witnesses.

But yet, if a Friend through tenderness have a desire that the magistrate should know it, (after the marriage is performed in a public meeting of Friends . . .) he may go and carry a copy of the certificate to the magistrate; Friends are left to their freedom herein. . . .

[Clearness for Marriage]

Let not any go disorderly together in marriage, contrary to the practice of the holy men [and women] of God, . . . when they took one another, all things being clear, and they both being free from any other, in respect to marriage. And when any take one another in marriage, let there not be less than a dozen Friends and relations present, . . . having first acquainted the men's meeting, and that they have clearness and unity with them, and then it may be recorded in a book. . . .

And all that are widows, who have children, and do intend to marry, let inquiry be made, what she hath done for her children, (if there be no will made,) then let such part of her late husband's estate be set out for the children, as is equal and according to truth; and what they can do more afterwards, let them do it also. And where there is a will made, let those legacies and portions be improved and secured (before their marriage) for the children of the deceased, with what more they can do for them. And then, when these things are done, let them be recorded in a book at the next Quarterly Meeting.

And all men that hunt after women, from woman to woman; and also women, whose affections run sometimes after one man, and soon after to another, and . . . after a while leave one another, and go to others, . . . these doings are more like Sodom than saints, and are not of God's moving nor joining, where they are not to be parted. For marriage is God's ordinance, and God's command one to another, and in that is felt the power of God. . . .

And take heed of hurting any concerning marriages, if the thing be right, (through any earthly reasoning,) lest they do worse. . . . And if any one hath any thing to say, in opposition to the matter of marriages, propounded by any to the meeting, such Friend or Friends to make it known, (what they have against the parties,) to such as are appointed by the meeting, to inquire into the clearness of the parties. . . . [Editor's Note: This paragraph is imported from Epistle 263.]

Now, no man ought to speak to a woman concerning marriage before that he hath spoken to her father and mother, and have their consent; and if she have no father or mother, but guardians and trustees, then they must speak to them, if she be under age. . . .

And you are to see, that every man and woman are free from all entanglements with any other woman or man before they are married; and if they have been engaged, you must have a certificate under the hands of the person that they have been entangled with to discharge them; so that all things may be done in peace, and unity, and righteousness, according to the truth that is in every man and woman. . . .

And if any man should defile a woman he must marry her . . . and condemn his action, and clear God's truth. But no such marriages, where the bed is defiled, we bring into our men['s] and women's meetings; but some Friends (if such a thing happen) draw up a certificate, and they to set their hands to it, that they will live faithfully together as man and wife, and fulfil the law of God. And this I write, . . . but I hope that Friends will be careful, and keep in the fear of the Lord, that they may have an esteem of the Lord's truth, and their own bodies, and of the honourable marriage, where the bed is undefiled.

[Friends Marriage Procedure]

And when any marriage is to be propounded, let it be laid before the women's meeting first. And after they have declared it there, if they do know any thing of the man or the woman, that it should not proceed . . . let them end it before it comes to the men's meeting; and if there be no such occasion . . . let two or three women go along with [the couple] to the men's meeting. And after Friends have taken their names, and places of abode, let two women of the women's meeting be nominated, and two men of the men's meeting, that if any one have any thing to say against the couple before the next meeting they may speak to them; and if there should appear any thing, they may end it before they come to the meeting.

And if there be nothing, when [the couple] come the second time again to the women's meeting, the women may go along with them to the men, and testify that they know nothing against their proceedings. And likewise the men that are appointed to inquire out to make the like report, (and let the man and the woman always appear together, when they lay their intentions of marriage.)

So then the thing is left to the men to give their judgment and advice to the couple that are to be married, all things being clear,. . . . then they may have their liberty to appoint a meeting where they please, in some public meeting-place, where their relations and Friends may be present, and there get a certificate ready drawn up, with the day of the month, place, and year, how that such a couple did take one another in the presence of God, and in the presence of his people . . . and all things being found clear, . . . to live together in christian, honourable marriage, according to God's ordinance and his joining, to be help-meets together as long as they live. . . .

That Our Lives May Preach: Accountability

Verily I say unto you,
Whatsoever ye shall bind on earth shall be bound in heaven:
and whatsoever ye shall loose on earth
shall be loosed in heaven.
Matthew 18:18 (KJV)

Settling Differences in Gospel Order (Epistle 264(b), 1669)

Introductory Note

These extracts about "Gospel Order" (which, in this case, refer to the Matthew 18 passage below) get to the essence of what Friends came to call "eldering." The first step, when conflict arises, is always to attempt to work things out in private conversation. Only then does Jesus say you can bring in others and finally bring the matter publicly to the congregation. It seems particularly important that Matthew 18:20 (which inspires the painting, "The Presence in the Midst") comes in the context of the authority of the monthly or quarterly meeting to exercise judgment when a Friend is reported to be "disorderly."

Note: After private attempts at reconciliation have been exhausted, Fox suggests that small ad hoc committees stand as mediators with authority to bring a decision. The principle involved is to avoid having controversy tear apart the community.

Scripture

Moreover if thy brother shall trespass against thee, go and tell him his fault between thee and him alone: if he shall hear thee, thou hast gained thy brother. But if he will not hear *thee, then* take with thee one or two more, that in the mouth of two or three witnesses every word may be established. And if he shall neglect to hear them, tell *it* unto the church: but if he neglect to hear the church, let him be unto thee as an heathen man and a publican. Verily I say unto you, Whatsoever ye shall bind on earth shall be bound in heaven: and whatsoever ye shall loose on earth shall be loosed in heaven. . . . For where two or three are gathered together in my name, there am I in the midst of them.

Matthew 18:15–18, 20 (KJV)

Epistle

Dear friends, if there happen any difference betwixt Friend and Friend, let them speak to one another; and, if they will not hear, let them take two or three of the meeting they belong to, that they may end it, if they can. And if they cannot end it, then it may be laid before the Monthly Meeting. And if it cannot be ended there, then it may be brought to the Quarterly Meeting, and there let it be put to half a dozen Friends, that they may end it. . . . Or, they that are at difference, may choose three Friends, and Friends may choose three more to them, and let them stand to their judgment: for there are few, . . . who will have their names . . . sounded over the country, that they are in strife; but will rather endeavour to end it amongst themselves or at their own meeting. . . .

And if there be any difference brought to the Monthly or Quarterly Meeting, . . . let but one speak at a time, know of them whether they will stand to your judgment? And, if they will, let half a dozen Friends make a final end of it. But, if they will not stand to your judgment, they are not fit to bring it thither.

And if any brother or sister hear any report of any brother or sister, let him or her go to the party, and know the truth of the report; and if true, let the thing be judged: if false, go then to the reporter, and let him or her be judged. . . .

Now concerning gospel-order; though the doctrine of Jesus Christ requireth his people to admonish a brother or sister twice, before they tell the church, yet that limiteth none . . . but that they shall not less than twice admonish their brother or sister before they tell the church. And it is desired of all, that before they publicly complain, they wait in the power of God to feel if there is no more required of them to their brother or sister, before they expose him or her to the church: let this be weightily considered.

And further, when the church is told, and the party admonished by the church again and again, and he or they remain still insensible and unreconciled, let not final judgment go forth against him or her, till every one of the meeting have cleared his or her conscience; that if any thing be upon any further to visit such a transgressor, they may clear themselves, that if possible the party may be reached and saved. And after all are clear of the blood of such an one [see Ezekiel 33:2–6], let the judgment of Friends in the power of God go forth against him or her, as moved, . . . that no reproach may come or rest upon God's holy name, truth, and people.

And all such as behold their brother or sister in a transgression, go not in a rough, light, or upbraiding spirit, to reprove or admonish him or her, but in the power of the Lord, and spirit of the Lamb, and in the wisdom and love of the truth, which suffers thereby, to admonish such an offender. So may the soul of such a brother or sister be seasonably and effectually reached. . . .

And be it known unto all, we cast out none from among us; for if they go from the light, and spirit, and power, in which our unity is, they cast out themselves. And it has been our way to admonish them, that they may come to that spirit and light of God, which they are gone from, and so come into the unity again. For our fellowship stands in the light, . . . and if they will not hear our admonitions . . . the light condemns them, and then goes the testimony of truth out against them.

And no condemnation ought to go further than the transgression is known; and if he or she returns, and gives forth a paper of condemnation against him, or herself, (which is more desirable, than that we should do it,) this is a testimony of his or her repentance and resurrection before God, his people, and the whole world; as David, Psalm lvii. when Nathan came to admonish him [see Psalm 51].

And that no testimony, by way of condemnation, be given forth against any man or woman, whatever crime they commit, before admonition, and till such time as they have had gospel-order, . . . according as the Lord Jesus Christ hath commanded; that is, "If thy brother offend thee, speak to him betwixt thee and him"; and if he will not hear, take two or three. If he will not hear two or three, then tell it to the church, &c.

And if any one do miscarry, admonish them gently in the wisdom of God, so that you may preserve him . . . from farther evils . . .; and it will be well for all to use the gentle wisdom of God towards them in their temptations and condemnable actions, and with using gentleness to bring them to condemn their evil. . . . So be wise in the wisdom of God.

And let no one accuse any one, either in a Monthly or Quarterly Meeting, publicly, except they have spoken to them by themselves first, and by two or three, as before. . . .

Papers to Disown Disorderly Walking (Epistle 220, 1662)

Introductory Note

Most meetings today are reluctant to exercise discipline, recoiling from the damage done by over-zealous elders in the nineteenth century. But for Fox, the purity of the fellowship—a social order of those governed by the wisdom of God—was of the essence of the gospel. Although still a practice among some Conservative Friends, writing a letter confessing fault will seem strange to most Friends today. If we no longer find this method useful, do we see some other process by which repentance and reinstatement can be acknowledged for those who "walk disorderly"? The point is not to do things "by imitation" but to see whether the old practices point to something suitable in our time.

Editor's Note: I have moved the sentence that begins, "If they will not write their own condemnation . . ." to a new location in this epistle that seemed to me to make more sense.

Scripture

Now we command you, brethren, in the name of our Lord Jesus Christ, that ye withdraw yourselves from every brother that walketh disorderly, and not after the tradition which he received of us.
2 Thessalonians 3:6 (KJV)

Epistle

Friends,—

> Truth is that which is pure,
> and is that which the serpent is out of;
> for there is no serpent in the truth,
> and it admits of no impurity. . . .
>
> So if any one have gone from it,
> they are for condemnation. . . .

If, among Friends, any reports or surmises be about any, . . . some of the faithful Friends of every meeting, whose sincerity is for the glory of God, his honour, and his holy name, . . . may be chosen to search out such things, and follow it till they find out the author or authors of it, . . . and the things that are for judgment, let them be judged and condemned.

And, if the report be false, let their innocency be manifest, and the reporter reproved. . . .

And furthermore, that Friends take notice of all such Friends . . . if they have any ways dishonoured the Lord God, and brought an evil report, either in their trading, lives or conversations, upon the truth; . . . that they may search into the bottom of it; that so, if they have done any thing worthy of condemnation and judgment, it may be [passed] upon them without any respect of persons.

And all Friends that have dishonoured God, and his truth, and people, and Friends have been to admonish them in a gospel-way, and they still go on in their wickedness and do not repent;

And, if they will not write their own condemnations, then Friends must write and deny them, and take it out of the mouths of the world.

Friends may draw up a paper at their meeting, (when they are clear of them,) against them and their disorderly walking, and unruly spirits, and looseness, in general words, not mentioning the particulars, except they be notoriously known. And Friends to do this with speed, and to bring it to the meetings; and if any one be known to be an open offender, that then there may be an open testimony against him in the particular; showing that we have no unity nor fellowship with such workers of darkness, and how that they cast out themselves from amongst us, being gone from the life and power of God; in which our fellowship is.

And that copies of the paper may be read in meetings. . . .

Send Reports to London (Epistle 253, 1667)

Introductory Note

This epistle, originally addressed *To Friends in Holland*, shows that, by the mid-1660s, Friends were beginning to keep records in London for both suffering and discipline for Quakers throughout the world. Some of these records were the papers of repentance or disownment discussed in Epistle 220. A central body of Friends in London would use a list of transient Friends who were "disorderly" to clarify that such travelers were not representing Friends. The accounts of suffering enabled Friends to more effectively lobby governments and particularly the English royal court for relief from persecution.

Note: Fox mentions "mittimusses and examinations." Mittimusses were warrants to seize and hold a person until examined by a court.

Epistle

Dear friends,—In the everlasting power of the Lord God I salute all the faithful and upright, among whom the Lord hath joy and delight. . . .

And so friends, all sufferings of Friends, of what sort soever, for conscience sake to Christ, in Holland, in Germany, in Zealand, in Gilderland, in the Palatinate, in Freezland, Sweedland, Switzerland, and Hamburg, send an account for what they have suffered, and by whom; together with the examples that are fallen upon the persecutors; with their mittimusses and examinations, send all these to London, to Friends there; that if any ambassadors or agents, out of any of those places, come to London, Friends may make application to them; for there are some Friends, who are ordered for the same purpose, to take knowledge of such things.

And likewise, if any Friends have come over into those parts of the world, and have . . . walked scandalously and disorderly; whether they have been such who have come over to minister, or seamen, and factors, or merchants, or masters of ships, whereby the Lord God hath been dishonoured, and . . . also all such who . . . have been deceitful in their callings, and have been exacters, and have not been true to their word; by such doings they cause the holy name of the Lord God, and his righteous truth, to be evil spoken of.

That a list of all such may be gathered up, and sent over to London, to such who are to receive them; and that if they condemn those things, and have given forth a paper of condemnation against them, if so, that we may have a copy of it also, to take away the reproach of their transgressions from Friends.

And let the faithful Friends amongst you meet together, to consider and take care about these things.

Do Not Tell Abroad Any Weakness (Epistle 256, 1668)

Introductory Note

In this epistle, Fox draws us back to first principles: when someone sins, the goal is reconciliation with God and the fellowship. To "not tell abroad" means, don't gossip, particularly outside of the fellowship. If someone repents, that need only be known where the sin was known because love cares for the reputation of others.

Scripture

Bear ye one another's burdens, and so fulfil the law of Christ.
Galatians 6:2 (KJV)

But above all thinges have fervent love among you:
for love shall cover the multitude of sinnes.
1 Peter 4:8 (GNV)

Epistle

My dear friends,—

Live in the wisdom of God,
which is gentle and pure from above,
and easy to be entreated;

all "bear one another's burdens,
and so fulfil the law of Christ."

And if any weakness should appear
in any in your meetings,
not for any to lay it open and tell it abroad,
that is not wisdom that doth so;

for love covereth a multitude of sins,
and love preserves and edifies the body;
and he that dwells in love dwells in God;
for God is love,

and love is not easily provoked;
and therefore keep the law of love,
to keep down that which is so provoked;
for that which is easily provoked hath words,
which are for condemnation.

Therefore,
let the law of love be amongst you
which is not easily provoked . . .
and so the body edifies itself in love.

Agendas for Monthly and Quarterly Meetings

Religion that is pure and undefiled before God and the Father is this:
to visit orphans and widows in their affliction,
and to keep oneself unstained from the world.
James 1:27 (RSV)

Let Nothing Be Wanting (Epistle 175, 1659)

Introductory Note

This epistle, originally entitled, *To Friends, to serve one another in love, in outward things, was subscribed, This is for the men's meeting*. It gives us a good idea of what Fox thought was the primary business of our monthly meetings. What would happen if the first item on our business meeting agendas was to "encourage one another to seek out the poor, and sick, and fatherless, and widow, and imprisoned, and make up their necessities and wants"?

Scripture

But by an equality, *that* now at this time your abundance
may be a supply for their want, that their abundance also
may be *a supply* for your want: that there may be equality:
As it is written, He that *had gathered* much had nothing
over; and he that *had gathered* little had no lack.
2 Corinthians 8:14–15 (KJV)

Epistle

My dear friends,—

In the order and wisdom of life
order all things to God's glory,
and dwell in the love of God together,
all serving one another in love,
and in the life of the truth;

and ye that "give to the poor, lend to the Lord,"
and he will give you again with advantage.

And so be fruitful in every good work,
and be subject to one another in the fear of the Lord,
and do that which ye do in love and peace;

and in that keep
in the authority and power of God,
in kindness.

And keep down and be master over all passion,
and the hasty and cross spirits,
and silence that which is sudden;
and let love have the pre-eminence
in all and over all.

And provoke one another to love and to good works,
and be diligent in all your places;
that ye may be a good savour in the hearts of all,
and that the truth may flow over all.

And let nothing be wanting amongst you,
and then all is and will be well.
And encourage one another to seek out the poor,
and sick, and fatherless, and widow, and imprisoned,
and make up their necessities and wants;
then there will be nothing lacking.

And keep in discerning, that ye may not be ensnared, nor made a prey upon; but that in the power and wisdom of God ye may be kept over all such, and to feel through all states and conditions. That the Lord God may be honoured in and by you all, and ye all may be preserved in his power and life to his glory.

For your bestowing of outward things to such as stand in need, is the least love, and things of little value in comparison to the things that are above and immortal. And so keep over all in that in which ye have the blessing poured upon you from the Lord God, to clothe and cover you.

Pure Religion Is to Care for the Poor (Epistle 264(c), 1669)

Introductory Note

The care for the poor—whether among Friends or in the wider community—is central to our Christian identity. We live in radically different social conditions than those Fox faced, but concentrations of wealth and poverty continue. What does this concern look like today?

Note: Fox suggests providing "a house for them that be distempered." Distempered can mean either physical or mental illness. The hope is the ill person will find better treatment among Friends than if they "go to the world."

Scripture

Neither was there any among them that lacked: for as many as were possessors of lands or houses sold them, and brought the prices of the things that were sold, And laid *them* down at the apostles' feet: and distribution was made unto every man according as he had need.

Acts 4:34–35 (KJV)

Epistle

And dear friends, in the power of the Lord God, you who are gathered with it, which is the authority of your men's and women's meetings; in the power of the Lord Jesus see that all things be well amongst you. . . . And that care be taken from time to time, as Friends are moved thereunto, for relieving faithful Friends' necessities, and for other services of truth, which shall be delivered into the hands of a faithful Friend or Friends, . . . who are to give an account of all monies, that shall be by them received and disbursed at the next Monthly or Quarterly Meeting . . . that ministering Friends may not be cumbered with outward things. . . .

And all Friends, be tender over all Friends that are prisoners upon truth's account, and that are sick and weak people, strangers and fatherless. . . .

And in all your meetings, let notice be given to the Quarterly Meeting of all poor Friends: and when ye have heard, that there is many more poor belonging to one meeting than to another, . . . let the rest of the meetings assist and help them . . . bear one another's burdens, and so fulfil the law of Christ. And so see that "nothing be lacking," according to the apostle's words, mark, "nothing lacking"; then all is well. . . . And amongst the christians in the first age, there was a men's meeting set up at Jerusalem to see that nothing was lacking, which was the gospel-order, according to the law of Jesus; and this continued as long as they lived in the life, power, and spirit of God.

But . . . the true church is coming up out of the wilderness, . . . and the marriage of the Lamb is come, and . . . the everlasting gospel is and shall be preached again, as was among the apostles; and the gospel-order shall be set up, . . . and a men's meeting, as was at the first conversion, to see that nothing be lacking in the church; then all is well. So there is not to be a beggar now amongst the christians, according to the law of Jesus, as there was not to be any among the Jews, according to the law of Moses. . . .

And now, that Monthly and Quarterly Meetings of two or three out of every particular meeting of true and faithful Friends are set up, . . . ; and by this you may come into the practice of the pure religion, which is to relieve the widows, strangers, fatherless, and helpless. . . .

> And Friends to have and provide a house for them that be distempered, and not to go to the world.
>
> And to have an alms-house or hospital for all poor Friends, that are past work.
>
> And Friends to have and provide a house or houses, where a hundred may have rooms to work in, and shops of all sorts of things to sell, and where widows and young women might work and live. . . .
>
> That all prisoners for the truth be minded, who are in want, and who are not, and the families of such who are in prison, whether they are in want or not; . . .
>
> and such as have left a calling, which they cannot for conscience sake follow; do the best you can to help them, and further them to employment, that they may . . . be a blessing in the creation. . . .

And all the fatherless children their estates to be recorded in a book at the Monthly or Quarterly Meeting; and all that are entrusted with any estates . . . to give an account. . . . And that every Quarterly Meeting may have an eye over such as are entrusted, and assist them in that which is right and righteous, and to see that they are faithful to their trust. . . .

And let two faithful Friends in the truth in every particular meeting be ordered to receive all collections, and to bring them to the Monthly Meetings; and let two such Friends receive them there, and bring them to the Quarterly Meeting; and let four faithful Friends receive them there. And . . . let an account be kept of what is received, and to whom it is disbursed; that so an account may be given to any faithful Friend that may desire it. . . .

And if any legacy be left by any deceased Friends to a particular use, as to putting forth apprentices, and breeding [i.e., "rearing and training," OED] of poor Friends' children, that the said money be kept distinct as a stock for the said use, and a particular account thereof to be kept; and the Quarterly Meeting to appoint some persons to receive the said money, and to keep the account thereof, and the meeting to see that it is disposed of to the uses aforesaid. . . . So . . . the memory of the deceased just Friend, that gave it, may not be forgotten. . . .

And all men and women are to order their children and servants in the order of the gospel, and in the new covenant, that they may all come to know the Lord. . . . And . . . the truth, and the light, and spirit of God must be walked in, which all looseness is out of. . . .

To All Women's Meetings: Go On and Prosper! (Epistle 320, 1676)

Introductory Note

Just as a primary agenda of monthly and quarterly meetings of Friends was to provide practical relief for the poor, so were they to provide a practical framework to support women in leadership and ministry. This epistle, which originally ran to nearly twelve hundred words, seeks to provide biblical proof for the equality of women and men in leadership and in holding separate men's and women's meetings. The epistle deserves study in full, and Jones, pages 326–339 provides a fine introduction. This much shorter extract celebrates the pouring out of the Holy Spirit equally on men and women, and concludes on a drumbeat of the equality of woman "as well as the men."

Here is an interesting footnote to Fox's argument for the legitimacy of women's assembling together in ministry. Fox notes that, when women gathered at the door of the Tabernacle, Moses did not say to them, "You are more fit to be at home to wash the dishes; or such-like expressions." Twenty-six years before Fox wrote that, in 1649, when he was twenty-five years old, this confrontation took place: the leadership of the socially progressive Leveler movement (many of whom later became Friends) had been arrested by order of Parliament. Large groups of women dressed in the sea-green color of the Levelers demonstrated raucously for release of the prisoners. A member of Parliament told the protesting women they should "go home and wash their dishes." The sergeant-at-arms told them to "go home and meddle with your housewifery"

(Healey:274). Perhaps that story still rankled Fox; perhaps "go home and wash dishes" was just a commonplace of patriarchy.

The original title of the epistle summarizes Fox's argument: *An encouragement to all the faithful women's meetings in the world, who assemble together in the fear of God, for the service of the truth. Wherein they may see how the holy men encouraged the holy women, both in the time of the law, and in the time of the gospel; though selfish and unholy men may seek to discourage them. But go on in the name and power of Christ, and prosper.* It is endorsed, *Marshgrainge, the 16 th of the 9 th month, 1676.*

Scripture

And it shall come to pass afterward, *that*
I will pour out my spirit upon all flesh;
and your sons and your daughters shall prophesy,
your old men shall dream dreams,
your young men shall see visions:
And also upon the servants and upon the handmaids
in those days will I pour out my spirit.
Joel 2:28–29 (KJV); c.f., Acts 2:16-18

Epistle

Friends,—

You may read [in Numbers 11:27–29] . . . when a young man said unto Moses, "Eldad and Medad do prophesy in the camp"; and he would have had Moses to forbid them: but Moses answered and said unto him again, "Would to God all the Lord's people were prophets, and that the Lord would put his spirit upon them.'"

So Moses here, (who was captain, governor, and judge over Israel,) was far from restraining any from prophesying in the camp, but . . . did moreover encourage them, by saying, "I would to God all the Lord's people were prophets:" and surely all the Lord's people are made up of both men and women. . . .

Now in the time of the law, there were the assemblies of the women; . . . as you may see in . . . [Exodus 38:8] the women's assembling at the door of the tabernacle of the congregation. . . . Now Moses and Aaron, and the seventy elders, did not say to those assemblies of the women, we can do our work ourselves, and you are more fit to be at home to wash the dishes; or such-like expressions; but they did encourage them in the work and service of God . . . both males and females. . . .

So you may see man and woman were meet-helps in paradise, before the fall; and . . . men and women in the time of the law were meet-helps again to one another. . . . And it is said, in Joel ii. and in Acts ii. "that the Lord would pour out of his spirit upon all flesh in the last days or times."

So this spirit being poured upon all flesh
in the christian times,

sons and daughters,
handmaids and servants,
old men and young men,

that by the spirit of God,
all these might have his visions,
prophecies and dreams:

and this is his spirit,
by which all should profit
in the things that be eternal,

and to serve God in the spirit,
both men and women,
sons and daughters,
old men and young men,
handmaids and servants;

all offer up to God his spiritual sacrifices.

For all being dead in old earthly Adam,
Christ, the heavenly Adam
has tasted death for them all,

and is a propitiation for the sins
of the whole world,

and he enlightens all,
and his grace hath appeared unto all,
and his spirit is poured upon all flesh,
and his gospel, which is the power of God,
is preached to every creature under heaven.

And now, must not all receive the grace,
and believe in the light,
and receive this gospel,
and walk and labour in it,

both men and women,
sons and daughters,
old men and young,
servants and handmaids[?]

Yea, I say,

the gospel being preached
to all nations, and
to every creature under heaven,

old men and young,
servants and handmaids,
sons and daughters;

I say, then

must not all these receive this gospel,
and the light and grace?
and are they not all to walk in it?
and to offer up their spiritual sacrifices
upon the heavenly altar,

in the new covenant,

and to walk in the new and living way;
and all to receive the light of Christ,
which enlightens all;

and to become children of light,
and to feel the blood of Christ
to cleanse them from all sin,
which they have in old Adam. . . .?

And some there have been, that would not have the women to meet without the men; and some of them say, the women must not speak in the church, and if they must not speak, what should they meet with them for?

But what spirit is this, that would exercise lordship over the faith of any? And what a spirit is this, that will neither suffer the women to speak amongst the men, nor to meet amongst themselves to speak?

But all this is for judgment. . . .

For the power and spirit of God
gives liberty to all;

for women are heirs of life
    as well as the men,
and heirs of grace,
and of the light of Christ Jesus,
    as well as the men,
and so stewards of the manifold grace of God.

And they must all give an account of their stewardship,
and are to be possessors of life, and light, and grace,
and the gospel of Christ,

and to labour in it;
and to keep their liberty and freedom in it,
    as well as the men.

And they are believers in the light,
as well as the men,
and so children of the light and of the day,
as well as the men. . . .

The Work of Monthly and Quarterly Meetings (Epistle 264(d), 1669)

Introductory Note

This set of extracts from Epistle 264 begins and ends with psalms that celebrate "the government of Christ." Fox sees Christ's rule expressed when men and women equally oversee the work and well-being of the church. The closing hymn celebrates keeping "the unity of [God's] everlasting spirit." The unity that may be found when a group attempts to discern God's direct guidance together is different in kind from the reasoned compromise of secular consensus decision-making.

Note: Fox says only "seasoned" Friends should participate in monthly and quarterly business meetings, but he also says, "The least member . . . hath an office and is serviceable." For the most part, Friends today invite all members and attendees into our business sessions as an expression of radical equality before God. Do we find any value in recognizing the presence of "seasoned" or "weighty" Friends among us?

Scripture

For though I be absent in the flesh, yet am I with you in the spirit,
reioycing and beholding your order, and your stedfast faith in Christ.
Colossians 2:5 (GNV)

And keep the order of the gospel,
the power of God,
which power of God was before the devil was,
and is over him,
which brings life and immortality to light
in men and women;

and men and women
they are to walk in this power of God,
and to keep in it, being heirs of the same,
and under the government of Christ Jesus,
who bruiseth the serpent's head,
and destroys him and his government;

men and women
being heirs of grace and life together,
and of the power of God,
and of the gospel of Christ Jesus,
the amen. . . .

my desire is,

that you all may be preserved in it,
to the glory of God,
and in his power, and light, and life,
over death, and darkness,
in the heavenly unity,
in all your meetings. . . .

So . . . the Quarterly Meeting should be made up of weighty, seasoned, and substantial Friends, that understand the business of the church; for no unruly and unseasoned persons should come there, nor indeed into the Monthly Meetings, but who are single-hearted, seasoned, and honest.

And if any one should speak or tattle any thing out of your Monthly or Quarterly Meetings, to the blemishing or defaming any person or the meetings, such are to be brought to judgment and condemnation; (for it breaks the privilege and order of your christian society in your meetings,) so that all may be kept and preserved in the power of the Lord, and in his spirit, in love and unity.

And therefore keep your meetings solid and sober, and let the authority of your men['s] and women's meetings be in the power of God; for every heir of the power has right to that authority, and in it keep the King of kings and Lord of lords' peace in his church. . . .

And the least member in the church hath an office, and is serviceable; and every member hath need one of another. . . .

And now Friends, so many Monthly Men's Meetings as you have in your county, you may have so many Monthly Women's Meetings; and if once a year, at least, you had a general women's meeting it would be well, (for in some counties they have as many Quarterly women's meetings as men's,) and in others they have only two, in the summer time, because the ways are foul and days short in winter.

And that one or two Friends in every meeting do take an account of all the marriages, births, and burials, and carry them to the Monthly Meetings; and let one or two there be ordered to receive them, and record them there in a book, which is to be kept at the Monthly Meetings. And from thence a copy of what is recorded there, to be brought to the Quarterly Meeting, and . . . record them all in one book, which is to be kept for the whole county. . . .

And that all Friends, . . . get decent burying places for your dead, and let them be decently and well fenced, that you may show a good example to the world in all things. . . .

And draw up an account of all that have died in prison, in every county, for truth's testimony, and lay them before the magistrates; and so to keep Friends clear from the blood of all men. And preserve a list of their sufferings, together with the number that have died in prison; that their blood may come upon them that have thirsted after it, and that their testimony may not be lost. . . . And so keep a record of them in your Quarterly Meeting books. . . .

And all my dear Friends every where, who have been moved of the Lord God to speak in steeple-houses to the priests, or in markets to the people, or in courts, or fairs, or assizes, or towns; let an account thereof be drawn up together in one book, with the substance of their words, that they spake in the power of God. This would be a book, that may stand to generations, that they may see their faithful testimony, and what strength God did ordain out of the mouths of babes and sucklings. . . .

And such testimonies of Friends as are deceased, let them be recorded. . . . [T]hey . . . carried on through great tribulations and sufferings; and many laid down their lives, and had their goods spoiled, and they persecuted to death, to keep up their testimony. . . . So that those words, that they were moved to speak forth by the power, may not be lost. . . . This may be easily done.

And all they that be public ministers, (if unknown,) that pass up and down the countries, and to other nations, for them to have a certificate from their meeting, where such persons are known, and all their practices are looked into; that will prevent any bad spirits, that may scandalize honest men. . . .

And, dear friends, be faithful . . . so that all things may be kept in that sweet order and government to the glory of God . . . that through the wisdom of God ye may adorn the truth in all things, for the preserving of love, peace, and unity amongst all. . . .

And my desire is,

that all the faithful men, and faithful women
in the light, and power, and spirit of Christ,
all may be kept in the possession of the truth. . . .

So that the joyful and glorious order
of the everlasting gospel,
all may be in the possession of;

so that in the light, spirit, and power,
ye may all have a care of God's glory,
and his honour, and his church's peace,

keeping in the unity of his everlasting spirit . . .
and so see,

that as every one has received
Christ Jesus, they do walk in him;
that all may walk in the holiness

which becomes the house of God;
so that God may be glorified by his light,
power, and spirit in all, who is over all,

God blessed for ever. . . .

Epistles in Numerical Order